T0316523

Cambridge Elements ☰

Elements in the Philosophy of Religion
edited by
Yujin Nagasawa
University of Birmingham

RELIGIOUS LANGUAGE

Olli-Pekka Vainio
University of Helsinki

CAMBRIDGE
UNIVERSITY PRESS

CAMBRIDGE
UNIVERSITY PRESS

University Printing House, Cambridge CB2 8BS, United Kingdom

One Liberty Plaza, 20th Floor, New York, NY 10006, USA

477 Williamstown Road, Port Melbourne, VIC 3207, Australia

314–321, 3rd Floor, Plot 3, Splendor Forum, Jasola District Centre, New Delhi – 110025, India

79 Anson Road, #06–04/06, Singapore 079906

Cambridge University Press is part of the University of Cambridge.

It furthers the University's mission by disseminating knowledge in the pursuit of education, learning, and research at the highest international levels of excellence.

www.cambridge.org
Information on this title: www.cambridge.org/9781108742238
DOI: 10.1017/9781108668224

First published 2020

A catalogue record for this publication is available from the British Library.

ISBN 978-1-108-74223-8 Paperback
ISSN 2399-5165 (online)
ISSN 2515-9763 (print)

Religious Language

Elements in the Philosophy of Religion

DOI: 10.1017/9781108668224
First published online: November 2020

Olli-Pekka Vainio
University of Helsinki

Author for correspondence: Olli-Pekka Vainio, olli-pekka.vainio@helsinki.fi

Abstract: What does it mean to use language religiously? How does religious language differ from our ordinary linguistic practices? Can religious language have meaning? Among others, these questions are part of the so-called problem of religious language, which originates from the peculiar object of many religious claims, that is, the transcendent, or more precisely, God.

Keywords: religious language, mysticism, positivism, fictionalism

ISBNs: 9781108742238 (PB), 9781108668224 (OC)
ISSNs: 2399-5165 (online), 2515-9763 (print)

Contents

Introduction

What does it mean to use language religiously? How does religious language differ from our ordinary linguistic practices? Can religious language have meaning? Among others, these questions are part of the so-called problem of religious language, which originates from the peculiar object of many religious claims, that is, the transcendent, or more precisely, God.

Logical positivism, a movement within analytic philosophy of the twentieth century, dismissed metaphysics and religious language as devoid of meaning, but this view was slowly discarded as logical positivism itself was abandoned as a self-refuting doctrine. This shipwreck rehabilitated metaphysics in the field of philosophy, and the charges of meaninglessness leveled against religious language were abandoned (Wolterstoff, 2009). The first section outlines the history and consequences of this particular debate.

Even if we could state that religious language may have meaning, many questions still remain open. The second section discusses properly theological objections to the use of religious language. For example, theistic mystical traditions (also known as "negative or apophatic theology") heavily restrict the validity of human concepts in spiritual matters so that human language can never capture God, who is incomprehensible. But how then should the use of language in the mystical context by persons like Pseudo-Dionysius the Areopagite or St. Edith Stein be understood? Negative theology is typically juxtaposed with positive, or univocal theology, or forms of analogical use of language, which claim that our words are directly applicable to the transcendent, or that there is at least significant overlap between our mundane use of the terms and their transcendent object. But how can this be the case if one still wants to maintain the radical otherness of God?

The third section discusses the nature of doctrinal language, including the examination of concepts such as metaphor and allegory. In addition, I will discuss more topical issues such as whether we should understand religious language as a "useful fiction," in what sense the theistic God is gendered, and whether multiple religions can refer to the same God?

My task here is purely descriptive, that is, I do not intend to suggest what religious people should think when they use religious language. Instead, I evaluate which available theories are good descriptive accounts of religious language, that is, whether they adequately explain what people are doing when they use religious language, or whether they are revisionary accounts that tell religious people how they should use religious language. Moreover, the aim of this Element is not to give a definite answer how we should evaluate the truth-value of religious claims. There are many other books that tackle this question directly.[1] Instead I hope to offer the reader tools that may help in understanding how religious language functions and how it sometimes may differ from other uses of language.

1 Language in the Search of Meaning

1.1 What Is Religious Language?

People have used religious language since time immemorial, yet there is no universally accepted definition of what counts as religious language. Also, as William Alston (1921–2009) has pointed out, 'religious language' itself is a misnomer since there is no language that is used only for religious purposes. Instead, there can be religious uses of any language so that a more correct term would be 'religious speech' or 'religious discourse' (Alston, 2004, 220). Sometimes theologians use the term 'God-talk' in this context. However, since 'religious language' has become a technical term in the philosophical literature, I will continue to use it throughout this Element.

What are the features that single out the use of language as religious? Obviously, sentences about supernatural beings can be religious, but not necessarily all of them. Consider two examples:

(1) God exists.

(2) God does not exist.

Let us assume that the first sentence is uttered by a theist, while the second is uttered by an atheist. The object of both of these sentences is God, who might or might not exist. We more easily admit that sentence (1) is religious while sentence (2) is not (although it could be if it was meant to express quasi-religious belief in, say, nihilism). Consider, then, this sentence:

(3) Forgive me, for I have sinned.

Again, this sentence may be religious or not, depending on the context and who utters it. A religious person may use it to express her guilt before God and neighbor, but she can also use the same sentence ironically to express her innocence in the face of false accusations. An atheist can use it to express his remorse without having any beliefs concerning the religious framework from which the sentence originates.

Therefore, it seems that we cannot decide whether a sentence is religious just by looking at the words and searching for their meaning in a dictionary

---

[1] See, for example, Craig and Moreland (2009); Evans (2010); Swinburne (2014); Plantinga (2015); Craig and Moreland (2009).

(Swinburne, 2008, 12–13). To offer some general definition, we could say that religious language consists of sentences that express some claim, belief, attitude, or preference which is religiously relevant. This definition can be taken to be too vague, but this is in keeping with the multifaceted nature of religious traditions, some of which are ambiguous concerning the existence of supernatural agents, for example. Also, the definition allows the possibility that atheists and agnostics may also use religious language.[2]

However, in this Element, I will limit my discussion to theistic traditions, and especially those sentences that make claims about supernatural reality, since this is the context from which the philosophical debate concerning the meaningfulness of religious language arose in the early twentieth century, and also because including nontheistic traditions would be too much for such a short Element. But let us now turn to the recent historical developments that created the so-called problem of religious language.

1.2 Ayer's Challenge

In 1936, Oxford philosopher A. J. Ayer (1910–89) wrote a small but influential book called *Language, Truth and Logic*, where he attempted, once and for all, to solve all great philosophical problems. His strategy was simple. Only those sentences that can be given an empirical verification are meaningful. According to him:

> The criterion which we use to test the genuineness of apparent statements of fact is the criterion of verifiability. We say that a sentence is factually significant to any given person, if, and only if, he knows how to verify the proposition which it purports to express – that is, if he knows what observations would lead him, under certain conditions, to accept the proposition as being true, or reject it as being false. (Ayer, 1952, 16)

Everything that does not fulfil this criterion is "literally meaningless."[3] Obviously to his mind this included statements concerning metaphysics,

---

[2] For example, Ian Ramsey (1957) makes a claim in his *Religious Language* that the proper use of religious language involves special discernment and commitment, by which he means some kind of conversion experience where the subject realizes the deeper and revolutionary meaning of particular words he has been using before without having the insight and illumination that reveals their deeper meaning. Ramsey's point here is the peculiarity of religious language when used by committed Christians and how in these cases the true meaning of the words cannot adequately be captured without special discernment. This is quite probably true, but some people may have atheistic experiences, which produce discernment and commitment of a different kind. Ramsey's model could be amended to include negations or denials of commitment as well, as I suggest here. Thereby, an atheist who denies the existence of God could also be said to use religious language. For a further discussion of Ramsey's model, see McClendon and Smith (1973).

[3] Of course, there is the class of analytic sentences, which surely have a clear meaning (like "all unmarried men are bachelors"), but these sentences do not add to our knowledge about the world.

aesthetics, ethics, and God. He admitted that there can be statements about morals, but these sentences are not factual like empirical statements. Instead, moral sentences (e.g., "murder is wrong") do not express a matter of fact but merely disapproval of a given action. Likewise, aesthetic sentences (e.g., "that painting is beautiful") express appreciation of the qualities of a given object. This view became known as *emotivism*.

Nowadays, philosophers generally think that Ayer's attempt to eradicate metaphysics with the help of the verification principle failed.[4] But why exactly? First of all, it did not take long for people to notice that Ayer's criterion itself fell outside empirical verification and into the basket of meaningless sentences. He tried to improve his theory in later editions of his work but was unable to offer a rebuttal of the criticisms leveled against his view.

Second, the problem with the verification principle was that all suggested criteria for it were either too strict or too lax. Either the principle itself could not pass its own test, or almost anything could pass it, including religious statements. This was due to Ayer's redefinition of his original principle so that even if some sentence A is not directly verifiable, it could be indirectly verifiable with the help of some directly verifiable states of affairs. This basically opened the floodgates since now we could put virtually anything into the basket of indirectly verifiable things and try to offer a justification with the help of claims that are directly verifiable. Of course, it is possible that the argument from directly verifiable things to indirectly verifiable things might be contested, but the fact that we are able to offer arguments for and against the success of these arguments and have a reasonable conversation about these arguments tells us that the line of demarcation between meaningful and meaningless sentences is more complicated than Ayer suggests.

Third, there is no evident way to sort claims as Ayer intended to do. Consider, for example, the following claim:

(4) It is wrong to torture people for fun.

This is neither an empirically verifiable claim nor just a matter of taste. Instead, it is a philosophical truth.[5] The ways we argue for philosophical truths are not

---

[4] For longer treatments of Ayer, see Scott (2013, 40–48); Weintraub (2003); Swinburne (2016, 24); Yandell (2013). Originally, Alonzo Church (1949) wrote a short but devastating review of the book, which many of the later critiques built upon.

[5] Here I have used moral facts to illustrate this strange nature of philosophical truths. In many ways, it seems that religious language behaves like moral language. Thus, for example, Ramsey (1957, 40–47) and Braithwaite (1971, 80). The difference between Braithwaite and Ramsey is that while Braithwaite seems to reduce religious language to moral language, Ramsey only argues that religious language bears a close resemblance to moral language without being reducible to it. Moreover, Braithwaite suggests that religious and moral language differ in the respect that religious language primarily consists of myriads of stories (which may conflict with each other)

empirical or scientific, although sometimes empirical states of affairs can be relevant for philosophy or theology, but there is not an a priori way to tell when this is the case. Of course, this issue, like all the other issues in philosophy, can be contested and debated. Even if we do not have a consensus view of moral language, the lack of it is evidence for not restricting options too soon and ending the debate.

Fourth, it is possible to formulate scientific hypotheses about unobservable entities, for example, multiverses, of which we currently have no idea how their existence could be reliably tested and verified. These theories are not nonsensical, and what they claim is understandable to anyone versed in the relevant literature. Therefore, we have good arguments against Ayer's view of restricting the realm of meaningful sentences as he does.

Even if Ayer got hoisted by his own petard, his ideas set the stage for the twentieth-century debate.[6] What kind of language is religious language, then? Michael Scott offers the following four theories that capture the basic options.

> *Face value theory.* Religious sentences represent religious facts and are conventionally used to express beliefs that those facts obtain.
> *Noncognitivism.* Religious sentences do not represent facts and are not conventionally used to express beliefs; they express noncognitive attitudes.
> *Expressivism.* Religious sentences do not represent religious facts but do conventionally express noncognitive attitudes; insofar as they represent nonreligious facts (if they represent any facts at all), they may be used conventionally to express belief in those (nonreligious) facts.
> *Moderate attitude theory.* Religious sentences represent religious facts and are conventionally used to express belief in those facts, and they conventionally express noncognitive states. (Scott, 2013, 9)

According to face value theory, the users of religious language use it more or less in the same way as any other form of ordinary language is used. It is factual, and it expresses beliefs. Noncognitivism fashioned according to Ayer's principles denies this and argues that religious language merely expresses noncognitive states, like approval and disapproval. On noncognitivism, religious

---

and that religious language somehow goes existentially deeper into the human psyche than moral language, being thereby able to motivate people to act morally, both outwardly and inwardly.

[6] Even if we could say that religious language is not nonsensical and it has a meaning, it may still be that religious language is incoherent. For example, I can say "the sum of the angles in a triangle is 280 degrees" and everyone knows what I mean to say, but the content of my claim is incoherent and obviously false. In a similar way, it is possible to claim that the way Christian theology defines the attributes of God is incoherent so that such a being cannot exist. This, however, is a completely different issue, which is concerned with the compatibility of theistic attributes. For a discussion, see Swinburne (2016).

language can have meaning, but the meaning is not objectively factual. Noncognitivism may sound like an atheistic theory, but things are not that simple. For example, many atheists affirm face value theory. They just think that the truth value of religious language is always negative: all religious claims are false statements (Dawkins, 2006). Ayer was an atheist as well, but he chose a different stance toward theistic claims: he thought that they are beyond verification and therefore more about subjective preference and not descriptions of factual states. While this, on the one hand, seemed to demote the public status of religious language, on the other hand, it opened a way to defend the meaningfulness of religious claims. This strategy became known as expressivism, which will be the topic of the next section.

The last view on Scott's list, moderate attitude theory, is his own preferred view, which is basically face value theory enforced with some elements of noncognitivism. Moderate attitude theory argues that the face value theory is basically a correct descriptive view of how religious people use language, but it acknowledges that religious language is not only about making factual claims, but consists of all kinds of possible speech acts. Religious language can be used to express nonfactitive states, such as prayer and praise and expressions of various emotions, like fear, anger, despair, sorrow, elation, hope, thankfulness, irony, exaggeration, approval, disapproval, confidence, and so on. Consider, for example, the following examples:

"I believe that God exists."
"God, why have you forsaken me?"
"I hope you can still forgive me."
"On the third day, Jesus rose from the dead."
"Thou shall not kill."
"If You are the Son of God, throw Yourself down."
"Faith is confidence in what we hope for and assurance about what we do not see."
"But the fruit of the Spirit is love, joy, peace, forbearance, kindness, goodness, faithfulness, gentleness, and self-control."

These examples show that religious language does not have easily defined boundaries. Nonetheless, the correct descriptive understanding of religious discourse and religious identity as a whole requires that at least some of the claims being made are not reducible to mere pro-attitudes.

Thinking about the following example might further elucidate this point. It is possible that a person (let's call him Sam) believes all the things a Christian should believe but fails to act according to his beliefs. In other words, he lacks a proper motivating element that is called a pro-attitude. On expressivism, religious convictions are interpreted as pro-attitudes so that when Sam says that he believes p, his belief that p can be conveniently translated into a pro-attitude so that it means "Sam is in favour of things related to p." Although no one denies that religious convictions sometimes involve pro-attitudes, they cannot be totally treated as *mere* pro-attitudes. Sam may have a religious belief of the following sort: "God loves human beings and expects humans to treat each other lovingly." However, Sam suffers from weakness of the will (*akrasia*), which inhibits his efforts to think and act lovingly. Sometimes he is so overtaken by akrasia that he simply does not care what happens to his fellow human beings. He does not call his mother as often as he should and pretends not to hear the pleas for help made by his friends, and so on. Yet he keeps on believing in God and the consequent moral ideals that flow from his beliefs. The example of Sam shows that it is possible to make a distinction between a belief and related pro-attitudes. Of course, this is not a paradigmatic instantiation of religious belief, but in Christian theology it is not uncommon to treat these kinds of instances where faith is somehow not perfect in every way as tokens of sincere yet imperfect faith.[7]

Other similar states that manifest the divorce of belief states and pro-attitudes are depression, apathy, outright rebellion, and irrationality (Scott, 2013, 55–56). Of these possibilities depression and apathy come close to akrasia as they can be ingredients in akratic attitudes. Concerning rebellion and irrationality, this is how the apostle James defines the so-called demon's faith (*fides diabolica*), which has all the propositional knowledge that genuine faith has, without the pro-attitudes, that is to say, demons have perfect knowledge of God, but not love for God.

> Jas. 2:19 You believe that there is one God. Good! Even the demons believe that – and shudder.

As already granted, these are not examples of what genuine religious belief should look like, but they nonetheless demonstrate that religious convictions cannot always be reduced to mere pro-attitudes.

1.3 Expressivism to the Rescue!

Even if Ayer's strict verificationism never carried the day, remnants of his thought continued to influence theological discourse. Ayer himself focused only on ethical language, which he defended with the emotivist theory, but he left religious language largely untouched. To fill this gap, the Cambridge philosopher and Quaker R. B. Braithwaite (1900–90) thought that maybe theological language, although void of meaning in an empirical sense, could

---

[7] On faith and the weakness of the will, see Saarinen (1994).

express something valuable in the same way as ethical language within emotivist constraints.

This gave rise to expressivism according to which religious language users are not asserting facts about the world but merely voicing out their preferences and plans of action. For example, when someone says before eating, "Come, Lord Jesus, be our Guest, and let Thy gifts to us be blessed. Amen," she is not asserting that a person exists referred to as "Lord Jesus" who visits us granting various gifts, but is merely expressing her general sense of gratitude for having something to eat ("Hooray! Food!"). According to Braithwaite, "the primary use of a moral assertion is that of expressing the intention of the asserter to act in a particular sort of way specified in the assertion" (Braithwaite, 1971, 78). For Braithwaite, when you scratch the surface of religious language, you will find moral language underneath. Religious language consists of stories about holy people, who are supposed to function as moral exemplars and sources and lead us to live sanctified lives. The point of the lives of the saints and all religious language is to guide believers to live "the agapeistic life," by which Braithwaite means life lived according to the highest moral ideals expressed in the aforementioned stories.

Also, religious belief is not doxastic, that is, it is not necessary that Christians actually believe the things they believe to be factually true or that the aforementioned stories in fact happened; instead "what is necessary is that the story should be entertained in thought" (Braithwaite, 1971, 85–86). The use of religious language effectively boils down to a useful fiction. Fictionalist accounts of religious language will be discussed in more detail in Section 3.

This reinterpretation of religious language was an apologetic strategy that tried to move religion away from the battlefield of public claims into the private sphere, where public verification did not pose challenges to it. Effectively, this would reduce religious language to noncognitive discourse so that there are no truth-makers in the world that make a sentence either true or false.[8] Braithwaite is quite open about his revisionist agenda:

> Stories about the beginning of the world and of the Last Judgment as facts of past or of future history are believed by many unsophisticated Christians. But my contention is that belief in the truth of the Christian stories is not the proper criterion for deciding whether or not an assertion is a Christian one. A man is not, I think, a professing Christian unless he both proposes to live according to Christian moral principles and associates his intention with

---

[8] A more recent proponent of expressivist account was D. Z. Phillips (1934–2006). Don Cupitt and his Sea of Faith Network (www.sofn.org.uk/) also has been promoting this view (Phillips, 1976, 2002; Cupitt, 1980, 2010).

thinking of Christian stories; but he need not believe that the empirical propositions presented by the stories correspond to empirical fact. (Braithwaite, 1971, 86)

Braithwaite takes the rigorous ethical demands of Christianity seriously but simultaneously thinks that there is nothing in the empirical world that grounds these demands. But is this a reliable way to interpret what the users of religious language are in fact doing and how the things in the world and moral obligations are connected? It seems not. Braithwaite's expressivism faces several serious challenges, which make it an unsatisfactory candidate for a good descriptive theory for religious language.

Michael Scott mentions several problems that are directly linked to Braithwaite's theory (Scott, 2013, 51–53). The problems originate from abandoning the view according to which religious sentences have a determinate meaning.[9] First, if the meaning of all Christian statements about God is agapeistic, this means that all Christian theological claims have one and the same meaning, which seems somewhat hard to accept. However, if one tries to avoid that consequence and claim that the meaning of the sentence is tied to the behavioral policy that is attached to a given sentence, we are faced with the situation where the same sentence can mean different things in different contexts. At this point, nothing separates religious language from Humpty-Dumptyism, which ironically was the position that expressivism tried to save religious language from.[10]

Also, more recent and developed versions of expressivism contain many problems that so far have not been solved. The most common criticisms are the following. First, the model is elitist.[11] It requires a very complicated state of mind, and many ordinary people, including many atheists, will find it unbelievable. Normally, people think that they should not believe nonsense or things that cannot be argued for using public criteria. Of course, often people do believe nonsense and form beliefs that have no justification, but hardly anyone would

---

[9] Braithwaite also leaves many things unsaid so that not all the consequences of his theory are as clear as they should be.

[10] Here's the famous exchange between Alice and Humpty Dumpty: "'I don't know what you mean by "glory,"' Alice said. Humpty Dumpty smiled contemptuously. 'Of course you don't – till I tell you. I meant "there's a nice knock-down argument for you!"' 'But "glory" doesn't mean "a nice knock-down argument,"' Alice objected. 'When *I* use a word,' Humpty Dumpty said in rather a scornful tone, 'it means just what I choose it to mean – neither more nor less.' 'The question is,' said Alice, 'whether you CAN make words mean so many different things.' 'The question is,' said Humpty Dumpty, 'which is to be master – that's all'" (Carroll, 2019, ch. 6).

[11] I grant that this charge does not prove the theory wrong. Many scientific theories are very complicated, and there are only a handful of people in the whole world who can understand, say, advanced physics. In this context, however, the elitism charge has some value because expressivist views are often offered as a way to fight secularism and make the religious way of life appealing to the masses again.

promote this as a good belief policy. It takes a lot of training to justify such an elaborate and counterintuitive view.[12] In fact, although some forms of noncognitivism are often offered as a kind of third way between theism and atheism, many atheists feel that noncognitive religious language is atheist by nature, having only an unnecessary and sentimental religious frosting from their point of view. The replacement of religious speech by secular language is quite easy and there is really no need for religious language. I will return to this issue in Section 3.

Second, the model creates an internal tension between users of the religious language: the representative of the noncognitive model must always remind other ordinary language users that they do not really know what they are doing. When ordinary people say, for example, "God is love," they are making realist claims, and from the point of view of the expressivist they are misusing language and stand in need of correction.[13] Ordinary users would agree with the expressivist that "God is love" means that "you must live agapeistically," but they would construe the meaning in the following way: "because God, who exists regardless of our faith and love, is love, we also need to act lovingly."[14] If the point of expressivism, as a revisionist theory, is to solve some of the problems related to public expressions of faith, it seems to create new problems within faith communities.

Third, on expressivism the meaning of religious language threatens to become arbitrary and only reflect the subjective desires of the people. This was the problem already noted in relation to Braithwaite. Some critics also speak of the "re-paganisation" of theological language (Long, 2009, 16). If there is little difference in the mode of speaking, it is possible to revive any old form of speaking or come up with a new one and suggest that language A refers to agapeistic life as well as language B. In other words, expressivism seems to make public discussion about beliefs virtually impossible because the meaning of the language becomes so elusive.

Fourth, noncognitive theories are unable to differentiate between various forms of religious language. Instead, they often put all their claims in the same basket and assume that all religious language is nonreferential. Thus, as a theory it is not well suited for making meaningful distinctions between ontologically different claims in the Apostles' Creed, such as "suffered under

---

[12] For an atheistic critique of noncognitivism, see Philipse (2012, 19–29).

[13] I do not claim that expressivists in fact go around correcting people, but they seem to have a moral obligation to engage in some form of corrective actions. See Cordry (2010, 85).

[14] How theists argue for their ethical views and their grounding is a matter of metaethics. For a discussion, see Ritchie (2012); Evans (2013).

Pontius Pilate," "rose from the dead on the third day," and "we believe in the forgiveness of sins."

Fifth, there are a number of cases of philosophical logic that manifest the problems of expressivism (Scott, 2013, 71–85). The so-called Frege-Geach problem, which concerns the truth-makers of complex sentences in different contexts, such as in the negative and in conditional sentences, is typically used to point out the difficulties in ethical expressivism (Schroeder, 2008). The same principles can be applied to religious expressivism as well. For example, think about the following sentence:

(5) Jesus rose from the dead.

An expressivist is supposed to give some noncognitive meaning to this sentence, which could be something like "Life prevails!" But consider, then, its negation:

(6) Jesus did not rise from the dead.

Again, an expressivist needs to come up with some noncognitive meaning of the sentence, but herein lies the problem. The meaning of (5) cannot be different from the meaning of (6) because then the sentences would contradict each other, and in order to contradict they would have to have a truth-maker, which is denied by expressivism.

Let us then think about the following conditional sentence:

(7) If Jesus rose from the dead, we will also rise on the last day.

What might be the noncognitive content of this sentence? It is important to note that this sentence could be uttered by both an atheist and a Christian. An atheist would mean that if Jesus rose (which she denies), then the general resurrection would follow. A Christian would mean that because Jesus rose (which she affirms), then we will be with him forever. However, there seems to be no noncognitive state of affairs into which the meaning of this sentence could be reduced. The same applies to religious questions:

(8) Did Jesus rise from the dead?

Like in the case of (7), there seems to be no obvious noncognitive state into which this sentence could be reduced.

Sixth, it seems that many religious sentences offer religious explanations of nonreligious facts.[15] For example, the argument from design intends to explain some facts about the natural world by referring to a supranatural creator (Sober,

---

[15] On how religious and nonreligious explanations overlap, see Legare and Visala (2011).

2019). The explanation itself can be formulated by believers and nonbelievers alike so that the sentences as such are not necessarily religiously relevant, but nonetheless design arguments may have religious relevance for some people. Claiming that religious language is not referential and expresses only noncognitive mental states does not seem to fit well together with these ways of using religious language. It can thus be concluded that expressivism is not a very good descriptive account of religious language.

1.4 Some Defeatist Options

If expressivism and all the other main options fail to convince, it is possible to try to deconstruct the whole discourse. The available options in this case are reductionism, subjectivism, eliminativism, or theological pessimism. Reductionism means that one denies the face value meaning of language A and argues that the truth-maker of the sentence can be found within language B (Scott, 2013, 121). Consider the following two sentences:

LANGUAGE A: God exists.
LANGUAGE B: Such and such natural processes exist.

The fundamental assumption is that the face value of the sentence in language A cannot be true. There is a class of sentences in language B that are not problematic like in language A, and there is both a way and good reasons to reduce language A to language B. Additionally there needs to be reason to keep on using language A instead of resorting completely to language B. Reductionism has been most famously supported by Baruch Spinoza and more recently by Gordon Kaufmann (Kaufman, 1981; Spinoza, [1607] 2007).

Reductionism works well with some religious sentences. For example, both A and B can be held true by a theist so that he thinks that B is one possible way to explicate the meaning of A. However, as noted, a reductionist would regard the face value reading of A as false. Things get more complicated with sentences that ascribe to God some great-making properties. For example, there are no good truth conditions that a reductionist could give to sentences like "God is righteous" or "God is all-knowing." Consequently, there is no choice but to judge sentences like this as false or nonsensical. Instead of being a theory about how religious language is used, reductionism seems to be a normatively revisionist theory as it proscribes how religious language should in fact be used and understood. If this is so, this threatens the whole reductionist project. Why keep using language that makes mostly false claims? As Scott (2013, 123) suggests, "a more philosophically respectable option for religious reductionists is to call for the elimination of the religious discourse and look to replace it with the reduced discourse." Eliminativism would be a position where one completely disregards the language A in favor of B. Some versions of reductivism look like fictionalism, which is the topic of Section 3.2.

Religious subjectivism falls prey to the same problems as reductionism. Subjectivist readings of religious language would locate the truth-maker in the language that describes my subjective feelings:

LANGUAGE A: God is love.
LANGUAGE B: God is love means that I have a feeling of love toward my neighbors.

A result of this move is that the meaning of religious sentences varies according to the context. Also, since the truth-maker is now the feelings of a given person, the sentence is always true, and if the person has appropriate feelings, people can never disagree about the sentence expressed in language A. This is a very counterintuitive result.[16]

The most radical option would to be to try to deny that human language is inherently incapable of uttering anything about God. This view is called theological pessimism: all speech about God is impossible. This might seem like an easy way out and a sure end to all religious disputes. Yet there is a problem, namely, the claim "No true statements can be made of God" requires at least one true statement of God, which is, of course, "No true statements can be made of God."

Why should we believe this statement? The background assumption behind the claim is something like this:

1. Language refers to the perceptible and experimental world.
2. God is different from the world.
3. Language cannot refer to God.

However, premise 2 can be interpreted in two ways:

2* God is not exactly like the properties of our world.
2** God is completely different from the properties of our world.

With some qualifications, we could say that Christians are more likely to accept the claim 2*, but not claim 2**. If one follows 2**, the only alternative to

---

[16] For a longer discussion concerning the problems created by subjectivism in modern theology, see D. S. Long (2009). He claims that the failure to retain a properly dialectical notion of religious language has several deleterious results. First of all, the attempts to remove God outside the realm of language will result in extreme fideism, where categories of public reason and evidence become unavailable for theology. Second, this demotes all God-talk to the level of ontotheology or anthropology. Third, all public debate concerning religion and belief will be about mere power relations, and as all means for rational evaluation of theologies have been removed (besides utility), the only mean left is coercion.

theology and religious traditions would be complete silence. But on what grounds would 2** be true? The obvious problem is that it seems to require at least some level of certain and undeniable knowledge of God, namely that the language cannot refer to God. But how does our theological pessimist know this, and can the claim possibly somehow be demonstrated to be true? Theological pessimists can invoke the diversity of God-talk for their support, in which case the debate moves to the question of whether the diverse forms of theology allow us to apply the categories of right and wrong to divine revelation.

In any case, in order to make the above statement about the radical difference between God and the world, a theological pessimist must assume that God and the world have at least one common characteristic:

> (A) The entity has a set of attributes that are not shared with any other entity.

While assuming the truth of A, the theological pessimist makes a true statement about God, while simultaneously denying that this can be the case. Thus, theological pessimism is unable to escape incoherence. However, a theological pessimist can try to mitigate his position and admit that there may be some potentially or even necessarily true claims of God, which, however, are quite abstract; for example, that "God is identical with his being." Still, a moderate theological pessimist needs to suggest that:

> (B) No essential attribute of God, such as goodness, knowledge, and power, can be the object of our knowledge.

How can we know this? To claim B to be true requires fairly extensive knowledge of God's nature, which, however, has been denied. Thus, the moderate version of theological pessimism is subject to similar objections as the stronger version.

A theological optimist thinks that 2* is a possible alternative. In this case, she assumes that God has become a "part" of this world, and there is no radical and absolute difference between God and the world. Making this claim requires a metaphysical theory that allows God's involvement in this world so that God remains transcendent but still somehow becomes available in this world. By availability, I mean things like God's revelation being of such a nature that it can be accessed through normal human cognitive processes and discussed using human language. Some Catholic theologians pursue this strategy under the technical concept of *analogia entis* (Long, 2011; Przywara, 2014). Contemporary Protestants, especially those who align themselves according to the theology of Karl Barth (1886–1968), typically prioritize the incarnation of Christ as the event that enables our words to refer to God (Johnson, 2010; Davies and Turner, 2002; Long, 2009).

2 Naming God in the Mystical Tradition

2.1 Aporia of Apophaticism

The previous section discussed the philosophical challenge to religious language, and now it is time to face the theological challenge. In theistic traditions, it is fairly common that some theologians and philosophers emphasize how God is transcendent, unknown, and ineffable. Here a typical distinction is made between kataphatic and apophatic theological traditions. Kataphatic theology (Gr. κατάφασις, 'affirmation') or positive theology uses positive terms to say something about what God is, while apophatic theology (Gr. ἀπόφασις, 'to deny') or negative theology uses negative terms to say what God is not.[17]

To get a grasp on how apophatic theologians restrict the access of human language to the divine we need to look at some examples. Perhaps the best-known apophatic theologian is Pseudo-Dionysius the Areopagite (fl. fifth and sixth centuries AD), whose work *Mystical Theology* had a strong influence on medieval theology.[18] This is how he limits our use of language in relation to God:

> Again, as we climb higher we say this. It is not soul or mind, nor does it possess imagination, conviction, speech, or understanding. Nor is it speech per se, understanding per se. It cannot be spoken off and cannot be grasped by understanding. (Pseudo-Dionysius, 1987, 141)

This kind of language is not only used by those theologians who are called "mystics." Here is an example from the most influential Western Church Father, St. Augustine of Hippo (354–430):

> Have I spoken of God, or uttered His praise, in any worthy way? Nay, I feel that I have done nothing more than desire to speak; and if I have said anything, it is not what I desired to say. How do I know this, except from the fact that God is unspeakable? But what I have said, if it had been unspeakable, could not have been spoken. And so God is not even to be

---

[17] Although negative theology has become the technical term to denote certain aspects of the mystical tradition, I have been told that a more accurate term would in fact be "a theology of excess." This is not to brush aside the methodological role of denial in the texts of Pseudo-Dionysius, but to place the denial in the larger context where denial is used to go beyond human concepts and images, which is underlined by the prefix 'hyper' in the beginning of Pseudo-Dionysius' *Mystical theology*: "Trinity! Higher than any being, any divinity, any goodness!" (Pseudo-Dionysius, 1987, 135). For other main figures in the western mystical tradition, see Sells (1994).

[18] Pseudo-Dionysius uses a pseudonym after Acts 17:34, where a Greek convert named Dionysius Areopagita is mentioned. Pseudo-Dionysius lived in the fifth and sixth centuries, and his true identity is unknown.

called "unspeakable," because to say even this is to speak of Him. Thus there arises a curious contradiction of words, because if the unspeakable is what cannot be spoken of, it is not unspeakable if it can be called unspeakable. And this opposition of words is rather to be avoided by silence than to be explained away by speech. And yet God, although nothing worthy of His greatness can be said of Him, has condescended to accept the worship of men's mouths, and has desired us through the medium of our own words to rejoice in His praise. For on this principle it is that He is called *Deus* (God). For the sound of those two syllables in itself conveys no true knowledge of His nature; but yet all who know the Latin tongue are led, when that sound reaches their ears, to think of a nature supreme in excellence and eternal in existence. (Augustine, 1958, 1.6.6 [*On Christian Doctrine*])

Protestant Reformers used similar language. Here is Martin Luther (1483–1546):

[God] is an inexpressible being, above and beyond all that can be described and imagined. (Luther, *LW* 37, 228, trans. Robert H. Fischer. WA 26, 339–340)

For if God's righteousness were such that it could be judged to be righteous by human standards, it would clearly not be divine and would in no way differ from human righteousness. But since God is the one true God, and is wholly incomprehensible and inaccessible to human reason, it is proper and indeed necessary that God's righteousness also should be incomprehensible. (Luther, 2016, 252 [*The Bondage of the Will*])

Remarks like these are not restricted to individual theologians but are also found in conciliar texts. For example, the Fourth Council of Constantinople (869–70) says:

We also know that the seventh, holy and universal synod, held for the second time at Nicaea, taught correctly when it professed the one and same Christ as both invisible and visible lord, incomprehensible and comprehensible, unlimited and limited, incapable and capable of suffering inexpressible and expressible in writing. (Tanner, 1990, 162)

The same sensibilities also occur in Jewish theology, where Moses Maimonides (1135–1204) is perhaps the best-known representative of negative theology. In his *Guide for the Perplexed* (ca. 1190), he writes:

If one describes God by means of affirmations ... one implies ... that he is associated with that which is not He and implies a deficiency in Him. (Maimonides, 1963, 1.58)

An example of a similar stance in medieval Islamic theology comes from the influential mystic Muhammed Ibn al-'Arabi (1165–1240):

It cannot be known through logical proof (*dalil*) or rational demonstration (*burhan 'aqli*), nor definition (*hadd*) grasp it. For He – glory be to Him – is not similar to anything, nor is anything similar to Him. So how should he who is similar to things know Him to whom nothing is similar and Who is similar to nothing? So your knowledge of Him is only that "Nothing is like Him" (Qur'an 42:10) and "God warns you of His Self" (Qur'an 3:28). Moreover, the Law (al-slar') has prohibited meditation upon the Essence of God. (Al-'Arabi, 2005, 33) (Quoted in Scott & Citron, 2016, 25)

These restrictions, which are not typical only for radical mystics, gave rise to a concern that was eloquently expressed by David Hume (1711–76) in his posthumously (1779) published *Dialogues Concerning Natural Religion* (4:1):

It seems strange to me, said Cleanthes, that you, Demea, who are so sincere in the cause of religion, should still maintain the mysterious, incomprehensible nature of God, and should insist so strenuously that he in no way resembles human creatures. I freely admit that God has many powers and attributes that we can't comprehend; but if our ideas of him are not, as far as they go, true and adequate and in conformity with his real nature, I don't know what remains that is worth discussing in this subject. Is the name, without any meaning, of such vast importance? And how do you mystics, who maintain the absolute incomprehensibility of God, differ from sceptics or atheists who assert that the first cause of everything is unknown and unintelligible? (Hume, 1998)

Of course, it would be strange to say that mystics, the highest rank among the religious, are in fact atheists.[19]

What is peculiar is that after restricting their use of language in relation to God, these same thinkers go on and write hundreds of pages about the very same thing of which nothing could be said. What explains this tension? Obviously, the mystics have something else in mind than denying *simpliciter* that nothing can be said of God. This basic intuition was expressed by Augustine in his *On Christian Doctrine* like this: "God should not be said to be ineffable, for when

---

[19] In fact, some years ago, it was debated whether Mother Teresa was in fact an atheist. This was caused by her statements that were prone to misunderstanding by those not familiar with the mystical genre. Consider, for example, the following account: "Lord, my God, who am I that You should forsake me? [...] I call, I cling, I want – and there is no One to answer – no One on Whom I cling – no, No One. – Alone. The darkness is so dark – and I am alone. – Unwanted, forsaken. – The loneliness of the heart that wants love is unbearable. – Where is my faith? – Even deep down, right in, there is nothing but emptiness & darkness. – My God – how painful is this unknown pain. – It pains without ceasing. – I have no faith. I dare not utter the words & thoughts that crowd in my heart – & make me suffer untold agony. So many unanswered questions live within me – I am afraid to uncover them – because of the blasphemy. – If there be God, please forgive me. – Trust that all will end in Heaven with Jesus. – When I try to raise my thoughts to Heaven – there is such convicting emptiness that those very thoughts return like sharp knives & hurt my soul" (Scott, 2016).

this is said something is said. And a contradiction in terms is created, since if that is ineffable which cannot be spoken, then that is not ineffable which is called ineffable" (Augustine, 1958, 10–11). In order to grasp what is happening in these texts, it is helpful to have a few technical terms at hand.

2.2 Univocity, Equivocity, and Analogy

When religious language is discussed, one always encounters these three terms: univocity, equivocity, and analogy. Historically, the modern use of the words originates from St. Thomas Aquinas' (1225–74) *Summa Theologica*, where he wishes to chart a middle road between univocal and equivocal predication. Here is Thomas's account at length:

> I answer that, Univocal predication is impossible between God and creatures. The reason of this is that every effect which is not an adequate result of the power of the efficient cause, receives the similitude of the agent not in its full degree, but in a measure that falls short, so that what is divided and multiplied in the effects resides in the agent simply, and in the same manner; as for example the sun by exercise of its one power produces manifold and various forms in all inferior things. In the same way, as said in the preceding article, all perfections existing in creatures divided and multiplied, pre-exist in God unitedly. Thus, when any term expressing perfection is applied to a creature, it signifies that perfection distinct in idea from other perfections . . . Hence no name is predicated univocally of God and of creatures.
>
> Neither, on the other hand, are names applied to God and creatures in a purely equivocal sense, as some have said. Because if that were so, it follows that from creatures nothing could be known or demonstrated about God at all; for the reasoning would always be exposed to the fallacy of equivocation. Such a view is against the philosophers, who proved many things about God, and also against what the Apostle says: "The invisible things of God are clearly seen being understood by the things that are made" (Romans 1:20). Therefore it must be said that these names are said of God and creatures in an analogous sense, i.e. according to proportion.
>
> Now names are thus used in two ways: either according as many things are proportionate to one, thus for example "healthy" predicated of medicine and urine in relation and in proportion to health of a body, of which the former is the sign and the latter the cause: or according as one thing is proportionate to another, thus "healthy" is said of medicine and animal, since medicine is the cause of health in the animal body. And in this way some things are said of God and creatures analogically, and not in a purely equivocal nor in a purely univocal sense. For we can name God only from creatures (Article 1). Thus whatever is said of God and creatures, is said according to the relation of a creature to God as its principle and cause, wherein all perfections of things pre-exist excellently. Now this mode of community of idea is a mean between pure equivocation and simple univocation. For in analogies the idea is not, as

> it is in univocals, one and the same, yet it is not totally diverse as in
> equivocals; but a term which is thus used in a multiple sense signifies various
> proportions to some one thing; thus "healthy" applied to urine signifies the
> sign of animal health, and applied to medicine signifies the cause of the same
> health. (*ST* I.13.5)

In sum, according to Aquinas univocal predication leads to inadequate speech about God since the terms cannot be applied in similar ways to God and created beings, while equivocal predication leads to an inability to say anything about God, and it is also performatively self-contradictory. Thomas's exposition may sound simple and straightforward, but this is not the case. He himself developed his views during his lifetime, and consequently later generations have had trouble interpreting him. In this context it is not apt to delve too deeply into the intricacies of medieval scholarship.[20] Nonetheless, Thomas is a good starting point for examining different possibilities.

Let us take a closer look at each of these options in Aquinas' list. A good example of equivocal theory is the Jewish philosopher Moses Maimonides. Like many other Jewish and Christian theologians, he thinks that God is absolutely simple and absolutely incomparable.[21] For Maimonides, the simplicity of God means that God does not have parts, and consequently lacks all intrinsic properties (Benor, 1995; Weed, 2018). Therefore, there is nothing in God that could be the point of linguistic reference. Maimonides' version of negative theology is quite extreme. All terms that we use of God and created things are completely equivocal so that there is nothing in common, except the name:

> Similarly the terms 'knowledge,' 'power,' 'will,' and 'life,' as applied to
> Him, may He be exalted, and to all those possessing knowledge, power, will,
> and life, are purely equivocal, so that their meaning when they are predicated
> of Him is in no way like their meaning in other applications. (Maimonides,
> 1963, 1.56)

Claims like these seem to create a tension with his insistence on the efficacy of theistic proofs that prove the existence of God beyond all possible doubt (e.g., Maimonides, 1963, 2.1). As Ehud Benor (1995, 347) points out, Maimonides' challenge is to explain "how thoughts and words can be about God if humans possess neither a description nor an experience of God." Maimonides attempts to do this by drawing a distinction between the reference of the name "God" and the conception of what God is. He argues that negative theology can help us to

---

[20] A good overview of Aquinas' thinking is Hütter (2011).

[21] The doctrine of divine simplicity is a much-debated topic in the history of theology. For a discussion, see Ortlund (2014); Duby (2016).

fix the reference without giving us the conception of God's nature. The negative theology Maimonides employs keeps him from attributing to God any positive properties or qualities, but this still leaves room for saying what God is not. Also, God performs certain actions toward the world, which can be referred to by saying things like "God is merciful." This, however, does not refer to the nature or essence of God, of which we can know nothing as such, but only to God's actions toward the world. Being absolutely simple does not rule out being able to produce multiple and varying effects that can be referred to. There may be room for some kind of analogical conceptualization of God, which Maimonides has to allow since otherwise he would be deemed to stay in complete silence. He claims, for example, that some proofs of natural theology (he was particularly fond of the cosmological argument) and that some analogies from the created world (he uses the unity of human intellect as an image of unity of God in Maimonides [1963, 1.1]) are valid.

Negative theology is best understood as a spiritual exercise, and as a theory of language and reference it is *sui generis*. Negative theology ensures that the worshiper does not worship an idol that is a figment of his or her own imagination. Maimonides argues that there is a difference between having a concept of God and directing oneself to God, and you can do the latter without having the former because negative theology carves out the place of God, of which nothing can be said.[22]

But does Maimonides' zeal to rid theology of idols lead to incoherence and impoverished notions of spirituality? This is the standard critique of negative theology, already noted by Aquinas, since the great theistic traditions typically

---

[22] There has recently been a growing interest among analytic philosophers to tackle problems related to apophatic theology, which have been mostly overlooked by the previous generation of analytic philosophers as obviously a self-contradictory project and not worth serious attention. Not only positivists but also Christian philosophers have offered strong rebuttals of at least some aspects of the apophatic tradition. See, for example, Plantinga (2000, 11–60). For an appreciation of the classical tradition, see Alston (2005). One recent contribution is provided by Scott and Citron (2016). One of their suggestions is that apophatic language could be seen as metalinguistic negation, that is, as a way of expressing unwillingness to use certain ways of speaking about God rather than rejection of the truth one has asserted. Thereby by relocating the discourse so that it is not about God (but about improper ways of talking about God) one is able to avoid the representation problem, which is the dilemma born out of the conjunction of the denial of language's ability to represent God while affirming that language cannot represent God. While this view may solve some problems and fit better with the intentions of some mystics more than others, it is questionable whether this suffices to depict the intentions of most mystical discourse, which at least on the surface level seems to be about God, not just about God-talk. For other suggested routes around these kinds of problems that rely on contemporary philosophy of language, see, for example, Kügler (2005); Lebens (2014); Keller (2018). Another solution is to see the apophatic discourse from a fictionalist or pragmatist perspective. The users of apophatic discourse know that their words fail to refer to God, but the actual point of using these terms is not successful linguistic referring but some other aim, like spiritual transformation. See also Ticciati (2013, 239–242); Yadaav (2016).

see themselves as founded on the historical acts of God, which actually tell us something about God. Of course, Maimonides allows the use of human concepts of God in spiritual practices while reminding us that the faithful need to realize that these concepts do not capture God. From this point emerges two basic traditions of spirituality. The first would say that these concepts do not capture God at all, and Maimonides seems to follow this route.[23] The second tradition would say that these concepts do not capture God fully, yet they tell something, fragmentarily, about God. This is the way of both univocity and analogy.

What worries some theologians with regard to univocity is the possibility of idolatry. By idolatry we mean, in most general terms, taking some creaturely thing and treating it as God, that is, misidentifying God.[24] This is how Richard Cross explains the dilemma of apophaticism and idolatry:

> Perhaps the alleged problem is that accepting univocal concepts requires accepting that God can somehow be grasped by the human intellect – and that this makes him less transcendent. I suppose we here bump up against apophaticism, and different senses of what it might be cognitively to "grasp" God. I am sure that the univocalist would want to say of God what we understand that God is good, and more besides, and that the univocalist would not want to say that God is merely the "more besides," and none of what we understand of what goodness is – which I take it is the burden of the serious apophaticist. But apophaticism as serious as this is not theologically required in order to maintain the distinction between God and creatures. After all, everyone agrees that creatures resemble God in certain ways, and in order to maintain the distinction between God and creatures, it is not required that we be unable to specify any of the ways in which creatures resemble God. (Cross, 2008, 192)

Univocity as such does not entail that one uses language in an idolatrous fashion. In fact, Duns Scotus (c.1266–1308), who was the most prominent defender of univocity in the middle ages, saw univocity as essential for philosophical and theological enterprise (*Ordinatio* 1, d. 3, pars 1, q. 1–2). If the concepts we use in theology and metaphysics cannot be applied univocally to

---

[23] In recent philosophy and theology, some forms of equivocity have been defended by some continental philosophers such as Jacques Derrida, Jean-Luc Marion, and Mark C. Taylor (Lewin, Podmore, and Williams, 2017). In these postmodern versions of mysticism, it is explicitly denied that religious language has a fixed reference point. Instead, it is the endless deferral of meaning that constitutes the spiritual journey. Nonetheless, even these forms of spirituality cannot fully escape the fact that in order to make equivocal claims one needs to say something literally.

[24] Idolatry is a sin that is often mentioned in the Bible; for example, in Leviticus 26:1–2, Isaiah 45:20, 1 Cor. 10:7, Rev. 9:20 (Tillich, 1957). A general definition of idolatry is provided by Robert Merrihew Adams (2002, 147) according to which idolatry is "'inappropriate love for excellent objects."

both God and creatures, theology becomes impossible, because we have no idea how the words are supposed to be applied. For Scotus, analogous predication as a theory is reduced to equivocity, although he does not deny the analogous use of concepts. The analogous use, however, is only possible because of an underlying univocity.

The fear of idolatry stems from the fact that now our concepts appear somehow to "capture" God, or that now some of our concepts (like 'being' when applied to both God and creatures) could perhaps be ranked higher in the chain of beings than God. However, nothing on Scotus' theory suggests that this would be the case. He subscribes to the idea of divine transcendence, according to which God and creation are divided by a metaphysical chasm. Univocity is for him a theory of how language and reference works (if it is supposed to have any meaning in the first place), not a theory concerning ontology (Williams, 2005; Cross, 2008; Horan, 2014).

In contemporary philosophy, William Alston (1989, 66–68) has defended "partial univocity." He argues, following Scotus' ideas depicted above, that there are cases when two things that are ontologically different can share some abstract features and this sharedness can be referred to linguistically. For example, I know that in this room where I now sit is a cat. If God exists, then he also knows that there is a cat in this room. In this case, we can use univocally the dictum "knows that there is a cat in the room" both in relation to God and to me, and in both cases the sentence is literally true, given that God exists. Of course, God's way of knowing exceeds the human way of knowing. Hence the univocity is only partial.

Additionally, Alston restricts partial univocity to functional concepts, which depict something that we, or God, does. It is therefore not possible to use the concept 'good' of God in a univocal sense, while it is possible to translate this as a tendency statement, like "God recognizes what is best."

Alston explains his stance thus: "The same functional concept of knowledge that p, or of purpose to bring about R, could be applicable to God and to man, even though the realization of that function is radically different, even though what it is to know that p is radically different in the two cases. We can preserve the point that the divine life is wholly mysterious to us, that we can form no notion of what it is like to be God, to know or to purpose as God does while still thinking of God in terms that we understand because they apply to us" (Alston, 1989, 71).

However, while being able to grant some form of univocity in religious language, the Alstonian version does not allow univocity in all cases. A possible critical response to this might be similar to the one made to Maimonides' model: these models of speech are too abstract and do not reflect the way religious language is being used in religious liturgy and spiritual life. Reducing the traditional great-making properties to tendency statements might sound bland. However, if one only wants to make a point about the validity of univocity in some instances of religious language, Alston seems to be right, and he does not propose that partially univocal concepts should be the only category one can use. Instead, "partial univocity gives us a secure foundation for the less determinate and explicit portions of our talk of God" (Alston, 2004, 242).

As already noted, Aquinas and many contemporary theologians claim that the best way to avoid complete silence and anthropomorphism is to claim that religious language is analogous. Despite its common use, the term itself is ambiguous. The magisterial basis for the idea was stated in the formulation of the Fourth Lateran Council (1215): "For between creator and creature there can be noted no similarity so great that a greater dissimilarity (*semper maior dissimilitudo*) cannot be seen between them" (Denzinger, 2012, 432). This, however, gives only a relatively vague definition for the idea (without even mentioning the word 'analogy'). The term 'analogy' comes from Greek philosophy, especially from Aristotle, who uses it as a tool to compare similarities between things that are "remote," that is, which are not alike and which cannot be compared with each other directly.[25] Analogy allows that one thing can be used as a model for another thing. The notion of analogy arises first within mathematics, and then it is applied to biology, theory of justice, theory of language, and metaphysics. The simplest form of analogy is the mathematical formulation $A/B = C/D$. This is extended to include the relation (R) so that $R(A, B) = R(C, D)$. For example, when we say that "fishbone is to a fish what bone is to a human," we do not intend to say that "fishbone is bone" but that in this specific context of comparison "fishbone has a similar function to a fish that bone has to a human."

So far so good. But how is this supposed to function in the realm of theology? Think about the following sentence: "God [A] is to the world [B] what an architect [C] is to a house [D]." We immediately see the difference between the sentence concerning various kinds of bones and the sentence concerning various kinds of creating. In the latter sentence, A is unknown to us, and we use the relation between C and D to attribute a creator/designer to the world since we know that houses also have creators/designers. Aquinas justifies this inference by the doctrine of causal participation, which means that creators always transfer something of themselves into their creations. Therefore, the things in the created world tell us something about its creator. This intuition seems to hold true with regard to simple objects like the sun and warmth, objects hitting each

---

[25] The history of the uses of analogy is provided by White (2010, 1–72); Ross (1981).

other at a certain angle and children looking like their parents. But when it comes to more complicated objects like houses, paintings, and symphonies, how much can we actually tell about Claude Monet just by looking at his painting *Impression, soleil levant* (1872)? Very little, I would say (White, 2010, 92–93).

The doctrine of analogy seems to give us very little knowledge about God. As it stands, this notion of analogy would amount to little more than agnosticism or a vague concept of some kind of designer. Aquinas, however, claims that we are not supposed to take human concepts and simply upgrade them to be fitting for the divine. A god that is merely an exalted version of something created is not God. Aquinas opposes univocal predication on the grounds that everything that is said to be common for God and creatures exists in God in a qualitatively, not only a quantitatively, different manner. Therefore, God's goodness is not only greater than the best form of human goodness, but it is perfectly instantiated only in God in a way that we can never fully comprehend. Instead, the primary use of the divine perfections, like love, goodness, and justice, is in relation to God and only secondarily in reference to creatures. Thus, human love is not a measure for divine love, but human love is something that only fleetingly and fragmentarily reflects divine love (*ST* I.13.6).[26]

I have already mentioned how grasping what Aquinas had in mind when he kept on reformulating his ideas of analogy is in fact quite complicated, and I cannot do justice to his thinking and various interpretations of him here. A concise summary must suffice. Aquinas distinguishes two types of analogy: analogy of proportion and analogy of proportionality. The former pertains to two things that have some determinate relation with each other. This type of analogy can be used to signify relations between creatures but it is inapt in theological signification. The latter pertains to two related things, like in the case when I say "I see a cat" and "I see that you are right" because seeing with my eye is analogous with understanding with my intellect. My eye is not my intellect, yet they perform to some extent similar functions (*De veritate* 23.7.9). Here, as Steven A. Long (2011, 47) explains: "we are speaking of the likeness of diverse *rationes* which do not fall within a determinate univocal order."

Now, Aquinas wishes to affirm that "we can name God only from creatures" (*ST* I.13.5). In a way this is almost a trivial point to make because our creaturely language is the only thing available to us. Yet this language fails us since, as Aquinas continues, "whatever is said of God and creatures is said according to the relation of a creature to God as its principle and cause, wherein all

---

[26] For a thorough exposition of how Thomas uses the tradition of divine names, which helps him to move beyond mere agnosticism, see D. S. Long (2009, 149–214).

perfections of things pre-exist excellently." We arrive at these perfections, or divine names, by first looking at our human concepts of perfection, and then proceed by removing all potentiality. In this way we arrive at *ipsum esse subsistens*, something that exists in pure actuality without any potentiality. This enables a true yet limited divine insight, which Steven A. Long (2011, 49) unpacks thus: "our knowledge is not knowledge of God's essence, but as it were true knowledge 'about' God's essence, for the truth of the human proposition that every pure or transcendental perfection belongs infinitely to God with no limit of potency whatsoever is not tantamount to the beatific vision. This does not mean that our statements are false. It means that the divine truth infinitely transcends the truth about God that we can cognize through human propositions."

The Swiss theologian Karl Barth (1886–1968) also acknowledges the need to apply some form of analogy when speaking about God. As a fierce opponent of natural theology, he rejects any attempts to move from the created order to the divine order by contemplation of the things of this world (Moore, 2013). However, he thinks that there are analogies of proportionality, which as relations are comparable to the divine (CD III/2, 220, 229). These include an earthly father's relation to his son as an image of the heavenly Father's relation to the Son, an earthly king's relation to his kingdom as an image of the heavenly King's relation to his creation, and so on. Barth has a very negative view of human reason in divine matters, and he insists that without divine illumination we do not even know what theological terms mean when we speak about God. Only after the revelation has been illuminated in our minds are we able to grasp the analogous nature of the human relationship as images of the divine. In Barth's case, analogy is something that we understand only after God has been revealed to us through special revelation, and only then do these analogies of the natural world have any value.[27] White explains this process of illumination in the following way:

> Learning the meaning of a word like "beautiful" certainly does not consist in showing someone beautiful things and being told that they are beautiful. It is a much more subtle process. To greatly simplify what actually happens, we may imagine the following. Suppose a child is shown a variety of things which he is told are beautiful. (The mother says "listen to the beautiful music" and so on.) Through this the child catches on to the word "beautiful." What does he learn? That these *are* all examples of beautiful things? Not necessarily. The mother might have appalling taste, and the examples for the most part be examples, not of beauty, but of sentimental kitsch. What will then be the case will be examples that *appear* to the mother to be beautiful. But it will

---

[27] For further discussion on Barth and Barthian traditions, see Johnson (2010); Long (2014).

also be apparent that the mother values these things and values them because she finds them beautiful. As the boy grows older, he may come to think that the things that his mother told him were beautiful were valueless, certainly by comparison with the things he now values. But he also recognizes those things that he had earlier been told were beautiful were caricatures of the real thing. That is to say, he learns the meaning of the word "beauty" from the fact that the things he was introduced to seemed to his mother to be beautiful, not that they were. In learning a word like "beauty," we can learn to see that those who use the word are putting forward things as meeting a certain standard – even if the things that they put forward fall far short of anything that is truly beautiful. In the same way we learn to use words such as "justice," "mercy," "judge" and "king" from their application to worldly phenomena and only subsequently, in the light of divine revelation, come to realize that these apparent exemplars are just caricatures of true justice, mercy, judgment and kingship. (White, 2010, 170, emphasis in original)

In the end, Aquinas and Barth are not necessarily that far from each other.[28] Aquinas' notion of analogy, as a form of natural theology, functions merely as a pointer beyond this earthly realm, and the actual theological content for the concept of God is based on special revelation (even if natural reason can also provide some proper theological content). Barth is more adamant in his opposition to all forms of natural theology that function without special revelation. Both of them, however, affirm the primacy of special revelation when it comes to spiritual knowledge of God, and they use analogy as a form of faith seeking understanding (*fides quaerens intellectum*).

2.3 Religious Language and the Mystical Ascent

Now we can take a closer look how negative theologians use religious language. It must be noted that each theologian has a particular approach and there is more than one way to draw everything together. Moreover, scholars have their own interpretations concerning particular figures, and the debate is ongoing. Here, I discuss how St. Edith Stein (1891–1942) explains the nature of mystical experience and our ways of speaking about God.[29] Stein's solution is of particular interest as she combines negative theology and Husserlian

---

[28] I realize that this is a strong claim that would require a lot of time to substantiate. The issue has been recently discussed in detail by an ecumenical group of theologians and their contributions are available in a collected volume. See T. J. White (2010). Also, I recognize that Barth himself never accepted the contemporary Catholic notion of *analogia entis*, even after extended discussions with Hans Urs von Balthasar.

[29] Edith Stein was born into a Jewish family, but in her youth she embraced atheism. As an exceptionally intelligent young woman she decided to pursue a career in philosophy, which eventually led her to become Edmund Husserl's assistant and the editor of his major works. During her studies, she converted to Catholicism and later joined the Carmelite order, where she became known as St. Teresa Benedict of the Cross. Stein was executed in Auschwitz due to her

phenomenology. Moreover, her thought is particularly stimulating as she approaches mysticism both as a mystic and as an academic philosopher who writes for a modern audience. Stein produced a number of works that are the subject of continued philosophical interest. One of Stein's lesser-known works is her commentary on Pseudo-Dionysius the Areopagite's theology, "Ways to Know God" (Stein, 2000b), which offers a clear exposition of mystical spiritual practices and how religious language works in this context.

In popular discourse, it is sometimes claimed that negative theology is the more sophisticated version of theology, while kataphatic theology is reserved for the uninformed. Based on this intuition, it is possible to formulate the following argument, which argues from the mystical experience of negative theologians to the impossibility of literal God-talk.[30]

Argument for ineffability from mystical experience
1. Mystical experience instantiates the highest point of spiritual life.
2. The mystic believes that his or her concepts are not capable of describing God; God is absolutely ineffable.
3. Therefore, the most advanced forms of Christian practice demonstrate how God cannot be referenced by means of human language.

A further practical conclusion can be drawn from 1–3:

4. We should not be too interested in how we speak about God. Instead, we should see our God-talk in a noncognitive fashion. Thus, it remains possible to use other, non-realist, options for God-talk. Furthermore, typical debates between theists and atheists are vacuous because they falsely interpret God-talk in a realistic way, that is, as referring to a factual state of affairs.

The argument aims to argue for absolute ineffability using reasons that are internal to Christian theology and practice. The force in this case lies in Premise 1, which refers to the "best of us." If such ones believe God is ineffable, we (the lesser ones) should adopt anti-realism concerning religious language as well. This issue relates to the theological problem of religious language: Are we trying to take God captive by way of our words? Furthermore, isn't the God we talk about using our fallible words necessarily an idol? Literal God-talk thus leads to spiritual failure, the critics claim (Westphal, 2001; Tillich, 1957; Hick, 2000). In technical terms this is known as the "ontotheological error."

Jewish origins. In 1998, Pope John Paul II canonized her and made her the patron saint of Europe (MacIntyre, 2005; Stein, 2010).

[30] The following argument is a formalized version of claims that several thinkers influenced by the continental tradition have made. See, for example, Knepper (2009, 2012).

Nonetheless, many scholars have claimed that literal use of concepts does not have this deleterious effect (Adams, 2014). Stein also shares this sentiment. According to Stein, both kataphatic and apophatic theology form the necessary basis for the movement of the soul toward the highest form of knowing, which is called mystical theology. The spiritual ascent is the result of the following process within so-called symbolic theology, by which she means the things one learns from catechisms and basic introductions to Christian faith. The symbolic theology, which can also be called revealed theology (in contrast to natural theology), is not supposed to be a mere object of philosophical speculation but an invitation to the specific dialectical process.[31]

Symbolic theology offers to the believer particular revealed concepts, which are then subjected to kataphatic and apophatic analysis. First, one affirms those things in creation that resemble God the most (like "love," "goodness," etc.), and then one moves to *via negativa*, which defines what God is not. This process helps the believer to move beyond the concepts toward the thing itself. Contrary to some popular ideas, apophaticism is not the high point of religious existence but only one of the elementary stages. Neither denial nor affirmation of the concepts and ideas of symbolic theology is able to reach its object perfectly, which is only possible for *theologia mystica* (Stein, 2000b, 116). As Stein explains: "Thus upon completing the ascent, positive and negative theology give way to mystical theology which in utter stillness enters into union with the Ineffable. The previous theologies represent stages leading up to the summit . . . although opposed, they do not exclude each other; they complement each other at all stages" (Stein, 2000b, 89).

In other words, kataphatic and apophatic theology are not successive stages but part of the same dialectic process, where they constantly correct each other. This process as such does not entail movement beyond words because it explicitly deals with words. Some forms of popular mysticism erroneously take silence and wordlessness as a starting point of spirituality, but that would be a grave misunderstanding of spiritual ascent as Stein describes it. Moving beyond words is a long and tedious process (Stein, 2003, 68).

Keeping with what was said about the inescapability of at least some extent of univocity in religious language, Stein seems to confirm this. Taking her cue from the famous story in the Old Testament (Ex. 3), where Moses meets God in the burning bush, she claims that "there is likeness, something objectively common, between the inexpressible thing that happened to him (Moses) and consuming fire" (Stein, 2000b, 97). In interpreting the linguistic elements of this

---

[31] For similar accounts, see also Ramsey (1957); Sonderegger (2015, 77–131); Long (2009, 168). Aquinas, *ST* III.9.2. resp. 3.

mystical experience, Stein argues that Moses' description of God as 'consuming fire' means, in the sense of partial univocity, that God has certain similar properties with consuming fire, even if God's nature is not exhausted by that which consuming fire is as a phenomenon in this natural world.

Here understanding the notion of analogy is of vital importance. Stein even argues that understanding the analogous nature of religious language is a necessary condition for being a Christian and without which one cannot help but embrace atheism (Stein, 2000b, 112; Stein, 2002, xxix–xxx). Analogy sets our language of God in its proper place: whatever we say about God, it is always subject to the rule "God is always ever greater." If this is not borne in mind, one lapses into either of two opposites, what Stein calls "Gnosticism" or "Paganism." By Gnosticism, she means equivocity where linguistic formulations always miss their targets. This accusation resembles the endless deferral of meaning (*différance*) as later defined by Jacques Derrida. Without a robust theology of creation and revelation this would in fact be the correct response, as then God would be totally outside of all human discourse. By paganism, she means univocity without a Creator-creation distinction, so that things in this world become deified, which effectively means falling into an ontotheological trap (Stein, 2000b, 119). In classical theism, God is not a thing in this world but being itself. Therefore, God cannot be found within this realm of being. Yet because of the recourse to revelation, Stein argues that God becomes available as a proper subject for human language but only in an analogous sense: God is something like this but always greater than we can imagine. But the fact that God is not ontologically on the same level with beings does not rule out, for Stein, that God is *to a certain extent* comprehensible.[32]

But is something lost when one moves beyond negative and positive theologies and receives a mystical experience? Here Stein uses Pseudo-Dionysius' words to describe what takes place at this level. Now God is experienced "inwardly without word and image" (Stein, 2000b, 108). What does this mean? I will approach this question by formulating two theses that relate to

---

[32] "Reason would turn into unreason if it would stubbornly content itself with what it is able to discover with its own light, barring out everything which is made visible to it by a brighter and more sublime light. For it ought to be emphasized that what is communicated to us by revelation is not something simply unintelligible but rather something with an intelligible meaning – a meaning, to be sure, which cannot be comprehended and demonstrated. What is communicated to us by revelation cannot be comprehended at all (that is, it cannot be exhaustively described by means of concepts) because it is in itself immeasurable and inexhaustible and at any time reveals only so much of its contents as it wants to comprehend" (Stein, 2002, 22). There is a long scholarly debate whether Stein's use of analogy is in fact more univocal than analogical in the end. See, for example, Przywara (2014, 596–612).

the argument for ineffability from mystical experience, and assess their respective strengths:

> Strong thesis: *theologia mystica* confirms absolute ineffability.
>
> Weak thesis: *theologia mystica* confirms that God is to some extent ineffable but expressions like "without words and images" refer to the lack of mediating representation, not to the falsity or inaptitude of our language.

The strong thesis would be in line with the argument for ineffability from mystical experience. Now, some of Stein's claims could be used to support Premises 1 and 2 of the argument even if Stein in fact follows the weak thesis. Stein uses apophatic language, which she inherits from Pseudo-Dionysius and which consequently allows for well-known radical interpretations.[33] However, Stein's analysis of Pseudo-Dionysius clearly makes her, and Pseudo-Dionysius as well, supporters of the weak thesis.

This is best explained by Stein's distinction between representations and the thing itself. The "inwardly without word and image" formulation does not mean that the words lose their meaning, but that they are not needed anymore (as representations) because the thing that has been referred to is itself present and gives itself to us without mediation. The difference between symbolic and mystical theology is in the role of representation. Symbolic theology is based on representations, whereas mystical theology involves the consummation of symbolic theology (Stein, 2000b, 95).

To offer an example: a teacher can speak about the Queen by pointing to a picture hanging on the wall. However, if the Queen enters the room, she does not need the picture to refer to the Queen who is now present in person. Also, the teacher's behavior will be markedly different in all respects in the latter case.

Furthermore, there is a direct continuum from the image to the original. A person who has been involved in symbolic theology, looking at the representation, will recognize the one represented to him through the images: "He alone can recognize *his* God, the God whom he knows personally, in the 'portraits'" (Stein, 2000b, 109, see also 96–97; emphasis in original). Thus "the images and words" are not considered ultimately false or misleading but they are *fulfilled*. If the movement from symbolic theology to mystical theology is an act of consummation, the movement from mystical theology to symbolic theology is an act of reduction that maintains the precarious link between these two worlds, without complete reduction of mystical theology to symbolic language (absolute univocity) and without claiming that nothing gets translated (absolute equivocity). As Stein writes, "What the prophet hears and sees is as it were

---

[33] For a concise summary and exposition of the thought of Pseudo-Dionysius, see Knepper (2014).

the great school of symbolic theology where images and words become available to the sacred writer so that he may say the unsayable and make the invisible visible" (Stein, 2000b, 108).

It is therefore possible to translate mystical experience into ordinary language so that it remains referentially true. Nonetheless, Stein hastens to emphasize that it is even more important to have this experience than to hear the prophets' words about it. If one receives this experience, she is able to "shape the image according to the original" and experience the consummation of the image.[34]

Finally, let me offer a perspective through Stein's early work on empathy, where she explains the meaning of empathy as follows (Stein, 2000a, 10): When we perceive "sadness," we first perceive certain facial expressions, but we move away from those to perceive the mental state that supervenes those facial expressions. Empathy, then, is a way of perceiving the world through the eyes of the suffering person and sharing her perspective, emotions, and experiences. The person is not empathetic if she concentrates on the facial movements and does not perceive the suffering that supervenes them. However, the observer would not be able to know that the other person is sad without those external signs. The external facial expression is not futile or misleading, though it is not the same thing as sadness.

The same applies *mutatis mutandis* to religious language and mystical experience. Symbolic theology, both in its negative and positive forms, is this external sign, which points toward something deeper. This does not make human religious language somehow deficient or misleading. Symbolic theology is the authoritative pointer that leads its practitioners closer to the things themselves. Staying at the level of natural or symbolic theology is, according to Stein, a sign of not understanding the role of symbols properly. It is like looking at the tears of a suffering person while forgetting the person.

Ian Ramsey has a similar view. He argues that theological concepts are infinite sequences that go on forever. In a similar fashion, there is no upper limit to the facts that we can learn about some person, and no matter how many facts we learn about her, this does not mean that we know this person or that we have established a relationship with her. This takes place only when we are properly introduced. Religious language functions in the similar way:

---

[34] Something like this has also been suggested by David Efird and David Worsley: "If we postulate that God is propositionally ineffable but personally effable, God remains both beyond (fundamental) description and beyond (fundamental) human concepts, in that knowledge of him can never be fully comprehended by or captured in (fundamental) descriptions or concepts, and in this way, the doctrine of divine ineffability can be upheld. Nevertheless, through some sort of intense second-personal experience at the beatific vision, God can still be personally known, fully and completely, just as we are taught in the doctrine of the beatific vision" (Efird and Worsley, 2017). See also Jacobs (2015).

> The first logical function of the word 'infinite' is to stimulate us to develop 'these stories of good lives' in the right direction. But in tracing such a sequence there is no intention of arriving at 'God' as a last term; the intention is to continue long enough with the sequence to evoke a situation characteristically different from the terms which preceded it; until we have evoked a situation not just characterized by a goodness which we admire or feel stirred to follow, but a situation in relation to which we are prepared to yield everything, 'soul, life and all'. Such a situation ... is often labelled 'Love,' but only when 'Love' has a significantly odd behaviour. For here is adoration, wonder, worship, commitment. (Ramsey, 1957, 68)

The movement from outward factual knowledge to personal knowledge requires "discernment" and "commitment," and this sets religious language apart from ordinary factual language. For example, stating that "the tomb was empty" does not function in the same way as "Christ has risen," even if their meaning is the same. Only when someone discerns the fundamentally odd nature of the empty tomb might she commit herself to the religious worldview this fact proposes.

3 Imagining God

3.1 The Nature of Theological Doctrines

Theistic religions claim that we can speak about God, because God has revealed himself. There are various ways how revelation can take place. In Christian theology, the following are typically listed among the sources of revelation:

- General revelation:
  - arguments from natural theology
  - conscience, or the natural knowledge of good and evil
  - providential events in the histories of individuals and larger groups

- Special revelation:
  - Religious experiences with specific content
  - Acts of God in history, especially in the history of Israel and the person of Christ
  - Sacred canonical texts

In these acts, God offers a point of contact from where humans can address God in God's own terms. This enables humans to form doctrines about God. In recent theology, George Lindbeck (1923–2018) has offered an influential model that helps to grasp the main options in the current debate (Lindbeck, 2007). In his much discussed book *The Nature of Doctrine*, Lindbeck introduced a distinction between propositional-cognitivist, experiential-expressivist, and cultural-linguistic views of doctrine. The propositional-cognitivist view, which Lindbeck associates with conservative or classical forms of theology, argues that doctrines are linguistic representations that make objective truth claims. The experiential-expressivist view claims instead that doctrines are linguistic interpretations and expressions of subjective religious experience. In keeping with the concept used earlier in this book, the propositional-cognitivist view would come close to face value theory, while experiential-expressivism is an obvious example of expressivism.

Lindbeck goes on to argue that both of these theories misunderstand how doctrines are in fact supposed to function in the lives of the faithful. Saying that doctrines make truth claims does not fully capture the practical function of the doctrines. Christians are not just supposed to say something that they think is true and leave it at that. Although doctrines make factual claims, they are more like action-guiding principles than mere observations about the world. This is better grasped by the experiential-expressivist side of the debate, which underlines the affective and practical elements of religious doctrines, that is, how they are made manifest in the lives of the religious. Nonetheless, the experiential-expressivist view also lacks something. Believers readily acknowledge that the beliefs they hold motivate (or they should motivate) them to act in certain ways. But they do so because they think that these beliefs are true in some stronger sense than just expressions of their emotions.

Lindbeck's own proposal, the cultural-linguistic view, tries to hold together the best of both worlds:

> Christian doctrines are not primarily either mere truth claims or expressions of religious emotions or experiences. Instead, becoming religious is to be understood more or less like accepting a normative worldview that is expressed in the doctrines. Here Lindbeck relies on Wittgensteinian notions of religious language as a 'grammar,' which provides rules for a specific discourse. All human activities are taken to be embodied by various grammars, which respectively shape each community, their beliefs and practices.

In his book, Lindbeck made a distinction between grammar as a second-order discourse and worship as the first-order discourse. His point was to underline that the liturgical practice is primary in the life of the church, and grammar is just a theoretical construal of this practice. In a surprising move, Lindbeck also argues that the doctrine (as grammar) does not make any truth claims about reality, but only about how concepts are used in the first-order discourse. He writes, "Just as grammar by itself affirms nothing either true or false regarding the world in which language is used, but only about language, so theology and doctrine, to the extent that they are second-order activities, assert nothing either true or false about God and his relation to creatures, but only speak about such assertions" (Lindbeck, 2007, 65). His intention behind this claim was to advance the possibilities for ecumenical dialogue between theological traditions. For example, Catholics and Lutherans had for a long time been separated by doctrinal formulations, which could now be interpreted as differing second-order grammatical construals of the same underlying reality.[35]

The Wittgensteinian theory that Lindbeck employs is called minimalism (Scott, 2013, 126–139; Stiver, 1996, 59–72). According to minimalism, religious language is propositional and it makes factual claims. However, these claims are internal to the discourse one is currently engaged in. Here a notion of a language game is frequently used to illustrate the rule-like behavior of languages. Using a language is like following rules of a game, and in order to keep on playing the game one must abide by the rules or start playing another game (often the rules are not made explicit, but they are nonetheless implied). It is the game and how it is played that tells you what the rules are and how they should be applied. This leads to the third point according to which there are different standards for truth in different domains of life. The standards of truth in physics vary from the standards in history, and aesthetic truths are different from religious ones. Minimalism differs from reductionism in that minimalists do not argue that we should reduce religious language to some other discourse, but they differ from face value theorists in that they deny that the criteria for truth are universal across the board of different disciplines.

While minimalism seems to get something right about religious discourse, it does not function well as a complete descriptive account of religious language. Minimalist accounts have trouble explaining sentences where religious language seems to reach beyond its own boundaries. This happens when religious language is used to explain something that is not inherently religious. For example, theistic religions contain many beliefs about the cosmos, its beauty and orderliness. Theists ordinarily use explanatory language that implies that the world is such and such because it is created by God. They also use similar language to voice their metaethical convictions saying things like "hate is wrong because God forbids it." As previously noted, it might be that these claims are false, but nonetheless this is the way people use religious language.

In several junctures, Lindbeck takes his cue from Wittgensteinian minimalism. In a famous example, Lindbeck tells a story about a crusader who strikes off the head of his enemy and yells "Christus est Dominus" [Christ is the Lord] (Lindbeck, 2007, 50). According to Lindbeck, the crusader's claim is in this

---

[35] This method is successfully used, for example, in *The Joint Declaration on the Doctrine of Justification* (1999) between the Catholic Church's Pontifical Council for Promoting Christian Unity and the Lutheran World Federation.

context false. Why so? Because the act of beheading provides the wrong kind of interpretative context for the claim. This performative understanding of religious truth has drawn charges of antirealism.[36] Why should we think that it is the crusader's cry that makes the sentence false, or why not think that it is the creed "Christus est Dominus" that makes the act of the crusader false (or morally wrong)?[37]

In order to tackle this question, Lindbeck distinguishes three kinds of truth: categorical, intrasystemic (coherentist), and ontological (correspondence). Lindbeck writes:

> It does no harm and may be helpful sometimes to speak of two other kinds of "truth," categorical and intrasystematic, that are necessary in order rightly to affirm the ontological truth of, for example, *Christus est Dominus*. First, in the absence of appropriate categories and concepts, Christ's Lordship is misconstrued. That Lordship is unlike any other: it involves, most astonishingly, the suffering servanthood of One who is God. Unless this is in some measure understood, "Christ is Lord" is false: it predicates the wrong Lordship of Jesus Christ. Nor does this proposition correspond to the reality affirmed by faith unless it is also, in the second place, intrasystematically "true," that is, coheres and is consistent with the whole network of Christian beliefs and practices. In the light of these clarifications, the tripartite division of "truth" implies neither relativism nor lack of objectivity. (Lindbeck, 2004, 15)

In other words, Lindbeck wants to broaden the act of reference in religious language so that it is not enough if one just says some words out loud. One needs also to practice what one preaches. According to him, this does not entail relativism or minimalism in its strictest form. He continues: "It most emphatically does not imply that the realities which faith affirms and trusts are in the slightest degree intrasystematic. They are not dependent on the performative faith of believers (as if, for example, Christ rose from the dead only in the faith of the Church), but are objectively independent."

3.2 Metaphors, Allegories, and Propositions

Many stories and images in the Bible seem to depict God in anthropomorphic terms, much like those in the Homeric tradition, where gods and goddesses were like elevated men and women. In contrast, there was a trend in Greek philosophy that attempted to offer philosophically more robust versions of

---

[36] More generally on realism and anti-realism in religion, see McGraw (2008). For commentaries on anti-realism in postliberal theology, see also Cathey (2009); Rauser (2009); McGrath (2002); Springs (2010).

[37] Thus, for example, Hunsinger (1993, 52); Hauerwas (2001, 176).

theology.[38] Early Christian theology had to confront this charge when philosophers of that time pointed out that the Bible contains a lot of crude and anthropomorphic imagery. For example, the opening sections of Genesis (1–3) speak about God walking, breathing, and even engaging in textile manufacturing. For the enlightened Greeks, this sounded too much like the gods of Mount Olympus, which had already been demythologized by the previous generation of philosophers.

The standard move in the face of these charges was to explain that these anthropomorphic passages should be interpreted in a way that was "worthy of God" (*axios tou theou*). In technical terms, this meant that the problematic passages were to be read as allegories.[39] As already noted, the early Church adopted the notion of divine simplicity that denied all composition and change in God, and allegory was seen as a good way to secure this idea: anthropomorphic images are human conceptualizations of how the immutable divine nature is related toward the world. However, no single theory was presented to decide which passages were to be read allegorically and which were the allowed interpretations (Sheridan, 2015).

Sometimes one hears contemporary theologians make a claim that all religious language is metaphorical. A radical version of this is *panmetaphorism*, according to which religious language is irreducibly metaphorical so that everything that is said about God must be said using metaphors, and the content of these metaphors cannot be expressed in literal terms (Alston, 1989, 17–19). Panmetaphorism is no doubt intended as a criticism of theological literalism, which takes depictions of God as literally true. However, from a purely philosophical point of view, there are some obvious problems with claims that argue for a purely metaphorical understanding of religious language. As Roger M. White (2010, 184; see also Long, 2009, 16–24) points out, theologians sometimes lack a proper theory of how these metaphors should be understood, so the appeal to the metaphorical nature of religious language is more reactionary than constructive.

Secondly, if we had a set of terms or a way of speaking that was genuinely and completely metaphorical, we would have no way of knowing what was being communicated to us. Namely, in order for metaphors to work, they need to have some kind of concrete reference point. The third problem with panmetaphorism is that while trying to avoid an anthropomorphic understanding of God, panmetaphorism is itself unable to escape anthropomorphic categories. If we are trapped within human language, then we are bound to use anthropomorphic concepts about something that extends beyond all human categories.

---

[38] For example, Xenophanes B16–23. Of course, this was an issue that led to Socrates' death (not believing in the anthropomorphic gods of the state).

[39] See, for example, Origen's comments on how to read Genesis in *De Principiis* 4.16.

Nonetheless, it is obvious that religious language is full of metaphors. So we need to ask, what kind of function do they have as a part of religious discourse?

Human language is messy and shambolic because it has developed in contingent interactions between individuals over long periods of time. Understanding language requires that one inhabits the space where the language is being used, and we need to understand the context and the history of the respective concepts. The language of logic, or the code of computers, is not like human language, and so far all attempts to translate human language into the language of our most developed artificial intelligences have failed for these exact reasons. Especially metaphors seem particularly hard to understand for our machine friends because they require massive knowledge about the context of the language. Unlike code, metaphors are not easily captured by strict rules. Moreover, our language is filled with dead metaphors, such as the word 'leg' to refer to "a leg of a table," "a stage of a journey," "a section of a cricket field," or "a courtly bow, where one bends one's rear leg while keeping the front leg straight." Sometimes metaphors ground the whole discourse, such as when things "run smoothly" or "flow." Here we are resorting to an underlying metaphor of 'river,' which is never explicitly mentioned (Stiver, 1996, 120; Soskice, 1985, 51).

Aristotle praised the use of metaphors in that they decorate language and make it more beautiful; however, they do not, he argued, add anything to what we know or what the lexical meaning of the sentence is. They simply stir our imagination by drawing attention to a similarity between two different things and then use descriptions in a surprising way based on recognized similarity: "Metaphor consists in giving the thing a name that belongs to something else" (*Poetics* 1457b1-30).

For Aristotle, metaphors were just ornaments of ordinary language. But often it seems that metaphors do express something more than just a similarity between two concepts. Take, for example, this famous scene from Shakespeare's *Romeo and Juliet*:

> But, soft! What light through yonder window breaks?
> It is the east, and Juliet is the sun.
> Arise, fair sun, and kill the envious moon
> Who is already sick and pale with grief
> That thou her maid art far more fair than she.
>
> (*Romeo and Juliet* 2.2.1–5)

Here Juliet, as the sun, is described as the most beautiful and commanding thing Romeo has ever encountered. We can unload the concept of 'sun' with a plethora of literal meanings without exhausting them. The fact that we understand what Romeo is saying entails that we recognize something similar between Juliet and the sun. Contra Aristotle, some recent theories about metaphors insist that as vehicles of speech they allow us to say something that cannot be expressed in any other way: metaphors are *irreducible*.[40] Moreover, instead of being mere embellishments that describe the world, they create and transform reality.[41] Metaphors can help us to see the world and ourselves in a new way. Perhaps one of the greatest examples of the use of metaphors was the prophet Nathan's allegorical speech to King David, where he uses a story of two farmers to expose David's adultery in 2 Samuel 12:1–13.[42]

William Alston points out that while there are a lot of metaphors in religious language, there are a lot of claims that clearly aren't metaphorical (Alston, 2004, 238). For example, when negative theologians say that "God does not have a body," this is obviously not a metaphor like all other negations in the mystical tradition. Secondly, the faithful can speak about God's actions in the world in the literal sense. For example, the sentence "God loves me and has forgiven my sins" is not a metaphor. To be fair, the object of this sentence is the

---

[40] Different versions of irreducibility have been defended by Paul Tillich (1957), Jacques Derrida (1997), Sally McFague (2013), and Don Cupitt (2010). On Derrida, see also Smith (2005, 54–60).

[41] For discussion of the development of theories of metaphor, see Stiver (1996), 114–115). Language captivates us, and from Plato (especially in *Gorgias* and *Phaedrus*) onwards we have heard philosophers warning us about the dangers of rhetoricians. Also, many great Western philosophers, such as Thomas Hobbes and John Locke, have castigated the use of metaphors in public speech on the grounds that they lead people astray and inhibit rational deliberation. Also, the contemporary movement of analytic theology shares a similar suspicion of metaphors. Michael Rea describes the method of analytic theology with the following tenets: "P1. Write as if philosophical positions and conclusions can be adequately formulated in sentences that can be formalized and logically manipulated. P2. Prioritize precision, clarity, and logical coherence. P3. Avoid substantive (non-decorative) use of metaphor and other tropes whose semantic content outstrips their propositional content. P4. Work as much as possible with well-understood primitive concepts, and concepts that can be analyzed in terms of those. P5. Treat conceptual analysis (insofar as it is possible) as a source of evidence" (Rea, 2009). Of course, none of this means that metaphors should not be used or that all of them should (or could) be reduced to literal language, only that metaphors should not be used in arguments if their use makes it harder to understand what is being said. See, for example, McCall (2015, 20–21). For an argument in favor of rhetoric in philosophical argumentation, see Warner (1989).

[42] ¹The Lord sent Nathan to David. When he came to him, he said, "There were two men in a certain town, one rich and the other poor. ² The rich man had a very large number of sheep and cattle, ³ but the poor man had nothing except one little ewe lamb he had bought. He raised it, and it grew up with him and his children. It shared his food, drank from his cup and even slept in his arms. It was like a daughter to him. ⁴Now a traveler came to the rich man, but the rich man refrained from taking one of his own sheep or cattle to prepare a meal for the traveler who had come to him. Instead, he took the ewe lamb that belonged to the poor man and prepared it for the one who had come to him." ⁵David burned with anger against the man and said to Nathan, "As surely as the Lord lives, the man who did this must die! ⁶ He must pay for that lamb four times over, because he did such a thing and had no pity." ⁷Then Nathan said to David, "You are the man!" (NIV)

event of forgiveness, which is partly my subjective state and also something that God does. It is not a direct statement about God's nature like "God is love." Since the former sentence is directed to the event and not God's nature, it is easier and unproblematic to treat it as a literal description of what has happened.

Alston also argues that metaphors, including religious metaphors, can be expressed, at least in part, literally in two different senses. First, there is some similarity between the two things that are being compared to each other. Second, the content of the claim can be stated by using specific propositional language (Alston, 1989, 23). To use Romeo's speech as an example:

> *Similarity*: There is a similarity between Juliet as the commanding center of my life and the sun as the center of our world.

> *Content*: Juliet is the most important thing in my life (i.e., the center of my world).

Therefore, it seems that claiming that metaphors in general and religious metaphors in particular are irreducible is a rhetorical overreach. It is no doubt true that some religious convictions are of such a nature that they are better expressed using metaphors, but this does not mean that they are irreducible.[43] That said, metaphors find their natural home in religious language because metaphorical expressions are well suited to the holistic role religious convictions play in the lives of the faithful. Instead of being mere statements of facts, metaphors are almost always specific speech-acts that either do or invite us to do something.[44] Paul Ricoeur and Ian Ramsey have underlined the revolutionary nature of religious language. Ricoeur speaks about "semantic shock" and Ramsey about "logical oddness" that shakes the listener so that one's perception is renewed. This often involves emotional, conative, and practical responses that shape both the intellect and will of the person, who is able to grasp the meaning of the metaphor. Jesus' parables often function as sorting tools, which are intended to separate those who understand the metaphors from those who do not.[45]

---

[43] For critiques of irreducibility, see Soskice (1985, 74–83); Stiver (1996, 130–131); Davis (1996, 62); Alston (1989, 17–37).

[44] I am not suggesting that propositions cannot do things and that this power is only vested to metaphors. Clearly, my statement "Bear!" is both a claim about things (a particular furry animal running toward me) that exist in this world and a commandment to flee or play dead, and some metaphors are 'dead' so that they still have the linguistic function but do not have the power many other metaphors have (like "a leg of a stool"). Mats Wahlberg offers an extended argument for why religious language cannot avoid being propositional at the core (Wahlberg, 2014).

[45] For example, Matthew 13:13: "This is why I speak to them in parables: 'Though seeing, they do not see; though hearing, they do not hear or understand.'"

3.3 Fictionalism

People engage in all kinds of matters they know to be not exactly true. Children play with dolls and pretend that they are real persons. Actors and actresses pretend to be someone else. Sometimes we get emotional due to what happens to characters in a book or in a play. Could religious language be taken to be an example of this kind of make-believe? A positive answer to this question is ordinarily called fictionalism.

According to religious fictionalism, it is permissible to participate in religious behavior and rituals, and to use religious language without believing that religious claims are in fact true. A further distinction is made between hermeneutic fictionalism and revolutionary fictionalism (Scott and Malcolm, 2018). Hermeneutic fictionalism means a stance from where one merely describes some state of affairs without any commitment regarding the truth of the matter. In these cases, a Christian teacher, for example, may use assertive first-person language to formulate, for example, creeds and beliefs of Islam in the classroom without herself sharing those beliefs.

Revolutionary fictionalists believe that we should think both that religious claims are not literally true and that we should nonetheless continue to use religious language and participate in religious activities without attempting to change them. The weaker version merely suggests that because we should be agnostic about religious claims due to lack of sufficient evidence, we are not entitled in believing in them, whereas the stronger version insists that we have good reasons to think they are in fact false, which makes believing in them epistemically vicious.

Effectively on fictionalism, it would be possible, and some argue that it would even be recommendable, for atheists to use religious language and behave in a quasi-religious manner. Why would an atheist do this? In the literature, the following arguments have been offered, which I have here split under three headings.[46]

Informative function
- Engagement with religious language and tradition helps people to better grasp the concept of the Good.
- Religious stories improve self-understanding and our knowledge of human interaction in general.

---

[46] The list has been collected from the following sources: Braithwaite (1971); Poidevin (1996); Eshleman (2005); Lipton (2007); Mill (1998); Sauchelli (2016); Scott and Malcolm (2018); Poidevin (2019).

Transformative function
- The use of religious stories has a morally beneficial effect on participants as it provides moral examples and elicits emotional responses, which may help one to act lovingly towards others.
- Engaging in religious rituals helps people to strive toward higher goals in life.

Aesthetic function
- Inhabiting a religious form of life enables a better grasp of the meaning and utility of religious art and aesthetics.

In these cases, one continues to use religious language, but one only quasi-asserts the religious claims.[47] One way of unpacking what this means is to say that one non-doxastically accepts the claims. This means that one may use the claims as a basis for practical, moral, and aesthetic reasoning without making a doxastic commitment about whether the claims are true. Non-doxastic acceptance has been defended by many philosophers and theologians, and it is generally accepted to be a state in which a believer may find herself occasionally, but it is not the paradigmatic version of faith (Audi, 2011).[48]

Another way is to say that a fictionalist merely pretends and engages in make-believe in order to gain some benefits, but this pretending does not guide one's life solutions beyond the sphere of the make-believe game and there is no incentive to develop toward doxastic faith.

Religious fictionalism confronts several challenges (Cordry, 2010; Pouivet, 2011). The first obvious question is: Does religious language offer such a way to achieve these aforementioned benefits that no other discourse can? It is not easy to answer this question because this depends to a large extent on the individual. For some people it may be that it is only religious aesthetics that does the trick. Nonetheless, it is at least possible that attending a nonreligious organization like the scouts, the Red Cross, the US Marines, or a political party improves one's life and morals significantly. Also, reading great literature seems to have

---

[47] In ethical discourse, one may hold a view called conservationism according to which one does assert that murder is wrong, even if one does not believe in moral wrongness. This move is argued on the basis of the utility of moral realist discourse over its alternatives. Also, to prevent the breaking up of interpersonal ties people may pretend to act in a religious manner. They push aside the epistemic considerations and cherish the social values that religious behavior, for example, during weddings and baptisms, encourages (Scott & Malcolm 2018).

[48] Christian tradition typically asserts its belief in an unashamedly realist manner. John Calvin writes in his *Institutes of Christian Religion*, "[faith] is a firm and certain knowledge of God's benevolence towards us, founded upon the truth of the freely given promise in Christ, both revealed to our minds and sealed upon our hearts through the Holy Spirit" (*Inst.* III.II.7) and Martin Luther writes "The Holy Spirit is no skeptic, and the things He has written in our hearts are not doubts or opinions, but assertions – surer & more certain than sense & life itself" (*De servo arbitrio, LW* 33:24).

beneficial effects for our moral transformation (Castano and Kidd, 2018). To illustrate what this would look like in a real conversation between two people, here is an excerpt from a dialogue between the famous atheist Christopher Hitchens and a Unitarian minister, Marilynn Sewell:

> **Sewell:** [. . .] I have my grandmother's Bible and I still read it, but I don't take it as literal truth. I take it as metaphorical truth. The stories, the narrative, are what's important.
>
> **Hitchens:** But then show me what there is, ethically, in any religion that can't be duplicated by humanism. In other words, can you name me a single moral action performed or moral statement uttered by a person of faith that couldn't be just as well pronounced or undertaken by a civilian?
>
> **Sewell:** You're absolutely right. However, religion does inspire some people. What about people like the Berrigan brothers, the Catholic priests who were jailed over and over again for their radical protesting of the Vietnam War? Or Archbishop Romero? These people claim to be motivated and sustained by their faith. Do you deny that?
>
> **Hitchens:** I don't deny it. I just don't respect it. If someone says I'm doing this out of faith, I say, why don't you do it out of conviction?[49]

Here Sewell is espousing something close to reductionism or fictionalism, while Hitchens is arguing for eliminativism. Sewell's argument seems to be akin to those mentioned before: religious language works particularly well as an ethical booster and therefore has some benefits over secular language, at least for her. Nonetheless, as a form of defense of religious language, this does not appear to be very strong. The argument could be weakened to state merely that for *some* people engaging in a religious form of life, while being an atheist, may result in various benefits, but this stance faces several additional problems.

The second question is: How does a fictionalist relate himself to the religious community, which does not think that fictionalism is true? At first, one needs to make a choice between different religious traditions. But by which criteria should this choice be made? It cannot be based on truth-value because the applicability of truth has already been rejected. This leaves only pragmatic ideals on the table. One should therefore choose that tradition and its beliefs, which helps him or her to achieve their goals. But here we see a possible conflict between the goals of the individual and the goals of the group. If the group finds itself in a situation where it is required to give an argument as to why it does X and not Y, it quite likely has a reason for it, which is not necessarily related to its pragmatic value. What does the fictionalist do in such cases? On the one hand, she can stay silent and exclude herself from the debate, which means that

---

[49] The whole interview can be read in: www.pdxmonthly.com/articles/2009/12/11/religion-god-0110.

she effectively identifies as an outsider. On the other hand, she can try to change the nature of the group so that it would become more fictionalist. This will change the nature of the group and quite likely cause a split within it.

The third question is: Is it ethical to engage in make-believe in cases where the make-believe may have negative consequences? This question relates to the point Hitchens made earlier. Why use a system that sometimes has good consequences but which is manifestly false, when you could rely on "convictions" by which he means secular humanist values.

The same questions come up in another dialogue between two philosophers, Nicholas Wolterstorff, a Christian, and Louise Antony, an atheist. Wolterstorff offered a reading of the parts in Joshua (6:21) where God seems to command the genocide of Canaanites.[50] One of his defenses is that as far as we know, this horrid incident never took place. What we have in the Bible is instead a rhetorical exaggeration of victory: a fiction of sorts. Antony does not accept Wolterstorff's reading:

> It's not at all clear to me that any good is accomplished by telling children things we know to be false, but which we pretend are true. Fictionalized history, it seems to me, is simply pernicious. It impedes true understanding. I have no problem with falsehood, *per se*; it's the pretending that disturbs me. Falsehood *per se* is called 'fiction,' and its forms include the novel, the drama, the fable, and the parable, all of which can be and have been put to excellent pedagogical use. (Jesus appears to have been a master of the last, as Wolterstorff observes.) [...] Either the falsity is essential to the edifying effect or it's not. If it is not essential, then we needn't continue to pretend. If it essential, however, then whatever 'edification' is achieved is illusory, for it depends upon a falsehood, and must evaporate if the falsehood is exposed. (Antony, 2010, 259)

I think Antony rightly points out that presenting falsehoods as true is pernicious. Of course, parents may fool their kids with Santa Claus, the Tooth Fairy, and the Easter Bunny, but these are harmless imaginative games. Things are more serious if we claim that things that ground our worldview are false and we choose to believe those anyway. However, some people may find themselves in a situation where they are agnostic, yet they hope that the thing in question would be true. If after careful consideration they think that worldview X is good and the likelihood of it being true is not too implausible, they are within their epistemic rights to accept it as a principle by which they choose to live in hope that they will gain more sound footing in the future, or if it fails, they recognize their responsibility to abandon it.

---

[50] "And they utterly destroyed all that was in the city, both man and woman, young and old, ox and sheep and donkey, with the edge of the sword."

3.4 Does God Have Gender?

Judeo-Christian theism typically addresses God with male pronouns.

> **Is. 64:8** But now, O LORD, thou art our father; we are the clay, and thou our potter; and we all are the work of thy hand.
> **Mt. 6:9** This, then, is how you should pray: Our Father in heaven, hallowed be your name [. . .]
> **Gal. 4:7** And because you are sons, God has sent the Spirit of his Son into our hearts, crying, "Abba! Father!" So you are no longer a slave, but a son, and if a son, then an heir through God.

Islamic theology does not have a similar emphasis on the fatherhood of God, and it has traditionally wanted to distance itself from the Christian conception of God as the Father of Christ. Nonetheless, male pronouns are used customarily to refer to Allah.

> **Quran 57:3** He is the First and the Last, the Evident and the Hidden: and He has full knowledge of all things.

However, both the Old and the New Testament contain female depictions of God.

> **Is. 66:13** As a mother comforts her child, so I will comfort you; you shall be comforted in Jerusalem. (See also Is. 42:14; 45:9–10; 49:16.)
> **Lk. 15:9** [Jesus said]: How often have I desired to gather your children together as a hen gathers her brood under her wings [. . .]

Nonetheless, Christian theology typically thinks that sex is a feature of a physical body. For this reason, angels and God, as immaterial beings, cannot be properly described with the category of biological sex. God is not essentially either a man or a woman (Num. 23:19). But if this is so, are not both masculine and feminine language equally apt in referring to God?

The Christian tradition, which follows Jesus' way and commandments (e.g., Mt. 11:27; Jn. 14:9) to address God as Father, is, however, more bound to using male pronouns for God, while emphasizing that this use is not literal but metaphorical. The univocal use of these descriptions would lead to an unorthodox view according to which God would have gender (Coakley, 2013, 248).

Although masculine vocabulary has been the default way of addressing God in the Christian tradition, this has not hindered theologians from doing justice to the analogous nature of theological language. Think of, for example, the Song of Moses (Deut. 32:6–18), where the author speaks about God using both masculine and feminine ascriptions. On the one hand, it is stated, "Is he not your father, who created you, who made and established you?," but on the other hand, "you were unmindful of the Rock that bore you, and you forgot the God who gave you birth." In this passage God is both father and mother, and the gender-exceeding nature of God is underlined in the disruptive metaphor of the rock that gives birth (Soskice, 2008, 79).

As an example from the later development of theology, here is the famous prayer of Anselm of Canterbury, where he addresses Christ as "mother."

> But you too, good Jesus, are you not also a mother?
> Are you not a mother who like a hen gathers her chicks beneath her wings? . . . .
> And you, my soul, dead in yourself,
> run under the wings of Jesus your mother
> and lament your griefs under his feathers.
> Ask that your wounds may be healed
> and that, comforted, you may live again.
> Christ, my mother, you gather your chickens under your wings . . .
> (Anselm of Canterbury, 1973, 153)

In examples such as these, the language is used in a peculiar way. Clearly, Anselm does not want to say that Jesus of Nazareth is not biologically male, or to claim that God is female. Both masculine and feminine descriptions of the divinity are best understood as analogies: God is to some extent like a human father or a mother. As Rea (2013) argues, masculine characterizations of God are no more or less linguistically accurate than feminine ones. From this, Rea concludes that it is morally permissible and liturgically appropriate to characterize God also in feminine terms. Rea bases his analysis on how accurate our theological descriptions are, and as far as this is the only criterion, his analysis seems to be right. However, theological language also has other functions besides accuracy. A deeper issue is the designation 'Father' as the name of God. In the Old Testament, God often stresses the importance of his name, which he will reveal to the people of the covenant.

> **Ex. 3:13–14** Moses said to God, "Suppose I go to the Israelites and say to them, 'The God of your fathers has sent me to you,' and they ask me, 'What is his name?' Then what shall I tell them?" God said to Moses, "I am who I am. This is what you are to say to the Israelites: 'I am has sent me to you.'"

This name does not as such include anything in relation to sex or gender. In fact, it seems to designate pure being in opposition to contingent creation. However, in the New Testament God reveals that his name is 'Father' (Lk. 11:2). Against gendered readings, it helps to put the 'fatherhood' of God in a proper category. 'Father' is not a description of sex or gender but a proper noun (Torrance, 1997; Kimel, 2001). Therefore, 'Father' is not purely a metaphor or analogy, even though 'fatherhood' works in these ways in liturgy and prayer (Ga. 4:6; Rm.

8:15). Also, it is not arbitrary, like the human names Eric or Janine, because it has a specific semantic content, which our names do not ordinarily have.[51]

3.5 Can Multiple Religions Refer to the Same God?

All theistic religions use the word 'God' to refer to the Supreme Being. Does this mean that they refer to the same entity? An important historical precedent for this question is Pope Gregory VII's letter to King Anzir of Mauritania (1096), where the Pope writes:

> God, the Creator of all, without whom we cannot do or even think anything that is good, has inspired to your heart this act of kindness. He who enlightens all men coming into this world (John 1.9) has enlightened your mind for this purpose. Almighty God, who desires all men to be saved (1 Timothy 2.4) and none to perish is well pleased to approve in us most of all that besides loving God men love other men, and do not do to others anything they do not want to be done unto themselves (cf. Mt. 7.14). We and you must show in a special way to the other nations an example of this charity, for we believe and confess one God, although in different ways, and praise and worship Him daily as the creator of all ages and the ruler of this world. For as the apostle says: "He is our peace who has made us both one." (Eph. 2.14) Many among the Roman nobility, informed by us of this grace granted to you by God, greatly admire and praise your goodness and virtues . . . God knows that we love you purely for His honour and that we desire your salvation and glory, both in the present and in the future life. And we pray in our hearts and with our lips that God may lead you to the abode of happiness, to the bosom of the holy patriarch Abraham, after long years of life here on earth. (cited in Neuner, 1982, 418–419)[52]

But what does it mean when the Pope says that Christians and Muslims "believe and confess one God, although in different ways, and praise and worship Him daily as the creator of all ages and the ruler of this world."?[53]

It is possible that two persons use differing descriptions to refer to the same entity (Kripke, 1972; Swinburne, 2008, 29). For example, I may use the words 'Bruce Wayne' to refer to the affluent bachelor holding a cocktail glass at a party. At the same time his butler Alfred Pennyworth refers to him with the word 'Batman' when speaking to Dick Grayson (also known as Robin). Both

---

[51] To be more specific, names often have semantic content, but nowadays proper nouns do not have this kind of function. For example, Peter means 'rock' (Lat. *petrus*), but few people think, when talking with someone named Peter, that this man must be a solid and trustworthy person.

[52] Thus also the *Catechism of the Catholic Church* (1.2.3.9.3): The Church's relationship with the Muslims. "The plan of salvation also includes those who acknowledge the Creator, in the first place amongst whom are the Muslims; these profess to hold the faith of Abraham, and together with us they adore the one, merciful God, mankind's judge on the last day."

[53] For general discussion, see Volf (2017).

Alfred and I succeed in referring to the same person. Could this example be used also in religious contexts so that different traditions would be speaking about the same thing? The problem with this suggestion is that we already know that Bruce Wayne is Batman. Do we know that Allah is the same God as Yahweh? This is something that the theory of description does not tell us, and it is something that needs to be answered by finding a way to compare what one believes about Allah and Yahweh. We would need evidence for the shared identity of these two entities, and only then could we say that differing descriptions refer to the same entity. This theory would then rely on a sufficient similarity between the descriptions of deities.

However, if we accept a nondescriptive theory of reference, then also people who have many false beliefs about God could perhaps refer to, pray to, and worship the same God. A version of nondescriptive reference is Alston's direct reference. In this case, the reference to God is enabled by one's experience of God, which is not dependent on a particular definition of God. This is also in line with many traditions of negative theology, which more or less say that our concepts do not accurately define God, so that all our speech about God is to some extent off the mark. Alston argues that this mode of reference has a dual advantage. First, it enables those who have not invested heavily in natural theology or philosophical education to refer successfully to God. Second, it allows that people from different faith traditions can be taken to be in contact with the same ultimate reality even if their descriptions vary (Scott, 2013, 104; Alston, 1989, 111–116).

It is beyond the scope of this Element to discuss global theologies of religions, so I will remain within theistic traditions.[54] By definition, theistic religions believe that there is only one God. As one Islamic Q&A website states: "Islam teaches that there is no 'Muslim God,' 'Christian God,' or 'Jewish God,' for that matter. There is only the One true God of the universe, the God of everything, living as well as non-living. He created all humans, whether they call themselves Hindus, Jews, Christians, or Muslims."[55] Basically Jews and Christians would affirm the same thing. There are no two or more Supreme Beings, which means we must be vigilant to which entity we refer.

From this perspective, it seems that as there is, according to the great theistic traditions, only one Supreme Being, and they may in fact refer to the same being because there is nothing else to refer to. Yet here we must remember that the

---

[54] For those interested in these matters, I recommend Veli-Matti Kärkkäinen's five-volume series, *A Constructive Christian Theology for the Pluralistic World* (Grand Rapids, MI: Eerdmans, 2013–17).

[55] http://aboutislam.net/counseling/ask-about-islam/god-male-female/

religious use of language is not interested merely in the question of reference. We can distinguish between the following forms of linguistic relationship:

- Reference
- Address/Prayer
- Worship
- Belief
- Knowledge

It seems possible that different religious traditions can in fact refer to the same God. It is also possible to address the same God in prayer (this is, in fact, necessary if there is only one God). They may even worship the same God, although this is not necessarily so.

For example, the Apostle Paul in his address to the people of Athens admits that they ignorantly worship the God he serves:

> **Acts 17:23** For as I walked around and looked carefully at your objects of worship, I even found an altar with this inscription: to an unknown god. So you are ignorant of the very thing you worship – and this is what I am going to proclaim to you. (NIV)

The word Paul uses here for worship is *eusebeia*, which means rightful spiritual reverence, the opposite of which would be idolatry. He does not, however, claim that all forms of reverence are genuine since he immediately disparages the worship of "gold, silver and stones – an image made by human design and skill." Theistic traditions believe many similar things about God, although they differ in their descriptions in important ways. The distinction Paul seems to be drawing here is that religious traditions differ in their manner of knowing but that it is also possible to worship something without knowing what or whom one actually worships. Consider, for example, the following account from the reformer Martin Luther's *Large Catechism*:

> These articles of the Creed, therefore, divide and separate us Christians from all other people upon earth. For all outside of Christianity, whether heathen, Turks, Jews, or false Christians and hypocrites, although they believe in, and worship, only one true God, yet know not what His mind towards them is, and cannot expect any love or blessing from Him. (*Creed*, 66)

Luther admits that theistic traditions believe in and worship the same God, but they do not know the same God. It is also worth noting that according to him also "false Christians and hypocrites" fail to know God. Luther's *Catechism* demonstrates that the common questions about reference and worship are not, from the point of view of religious practice, the most important questions. Nonetheless, the examination of theories of reference can aid faith traditions when they enter into dialogue to find common ground. For many religions and worldviews both the content of belief and the manner of believing is important, and these questions should not be overlooked. These questions, however, ultimately reach deeper than how language works, and enter another realm, where it is asked what a given religious language implies as a form of life.

Abbreviations

CD	Barth, Karl. *Church Dogmatics.*
Engl.	English
Gr.	Greek
Lat.	Latin
LW	Luther, Martin. *Luther's Works.* American Edition. Philadelphia: Fortress Press, 1955–86.
NIV	New International Version.
Ord.	Scotus, *Ordinatio. Opera omnia.* Edited by The Scotistic Commission. Vatican City: Typis Vaticanis, 1950–.
ST	Thomas Aquinas, *Summa Theologiae.* Fathers of the English Dominican Province Translation. Online www.documentacatholicaomnia.eu////03d//1225-1274,_Thomas_Aquinas,_Summa_Theologiae_%5B1%5D,_EN.pdf
WA	Luther, Martin. *Werke. Weimarer Ausgabe.* Weimar: Bohlau, 1883–.

Bibliography

Adams, M. M. (2014) "What's Wrong with the Ontotheological Error?," *Journal of Analytic Theology*, 2(1), pp. 1–12. doi:10.12978/jat.2014-1.120013000318a.

Adams, R. M. (2002) *Finite and Infinite Goods*. Oxford: Oxford University Press.

Al-'Arabi, M. I. (2005) *Meccan Revelations vol. 1*. New York: Pir Press.

Alston, W. (1989) *Divine Nature and Human Language. Essays in Philosophical Theology*. Ithaca, NY: Cornell University Press.

Alston, W. (2004) "Religious Language," in Wainwright, W. J. (ed.) *The Oxford Handbook of Philosophy of Religion*. Oxford: Oxford University Press, pp. 220–245.

Alston, W. (2005) "Two Cheers for Mystery!," in Dole, A. and Chignell, A. (eds.) *God and the Ethics of Belief*. Cambridge: Cambridge University Press, pp. 99–116.

Antony, L. (2010) "Comments on Reading Joshua," in Bergman, M. (ed.) *Divine Evil*. Oxford: Oxford University Press.

Audi, R. (2011) *Rationality and Religious Commitment*. Oxford: Oxford University Press.

Augustine (1958) *On Christian Doctrine*. Tr. by D. W. Robertson Jr. London: Macmillan.

Ayer, A. J. (1952) *Language, Truth and Logic*. London: Dover Publications.

Barth, K. (2010) *Church Dogmatics III.2: The Doctrine of Creation*. London: T&T Clark International.

Benor, E. Z. (1995) "Meaning and Reference in Maimonides' Negative Theology," *The Harvard Theological Review*, 88(3), pp. 339–360.

Braithwaite, R. B. (1971) "An Empiricist's View of the Nature of Religious Belief [1955]," in Mitchell, B. (ed.) *Philosophy of Religion*. Oxford: Oxford University Press, pp. 72–91.

Canterbury, A. of (1973) *The Prayers and Meditations of St. Anselm*. Translated by S. Benedicta Ward. New York: Penguin.

Carroll, L. (2019) *Through the Looking Glass*. London: SDE Classics.

Castano, E., and Kidd, D. (2018) "Reading Literary Fiction Can Improve Theory of Mind," *Nature Human Behaviour*, 2, p. 604.

Cathey, R. A. (2009) *God in Postliberal Perspective. Between Realism and Non-Realism*. Aldershot: Ashgate.

Church, A. (1949) "Review: Alfred Jules Ayer, Language, Truth and Logic," *Journal of Symbolic Logic*, 14(1), pp. 52–53.

Coakley, S. (2013) *God, Sexuality and the Self.* Cambridge: Cambridge University Press.

Cordry, B. S. (2010) "A Critique of Religious Fictionalism," *Religious Studies*, 46(1), pp. 77–89.

Craig, W. L., and Moreland, J. P. (2009) *The Blackwell Companion to Natural Theology.* Malden, MA: Wiley-Blackwell.

Cross, R. (2008) "Idolatry and Religious Language," *Faith and Philosophy*, 25(2), pp. 190–196.

Cupitt, D. (1980) *Taking Leave of God.* London: SCM Press.

Cupitt, D. (2010) *The Fountain: A Secular Theology.* London: SCM Press.

Davies, O., and Turner, D. (eds.) (2002) *Silence and the Word: Negative Theology and Incarnation.* Cambridge: Cambridge University Press.

Davis, S. T. (1996) *Christian Philosophical Theology.* Oxford: Oxford University Press.

Dawkins, R. (2006) *The God Delusion.* Boston: Houghton Mifflin Co.

Denzinger, H. (2012) *Compendium of Creeds, Definitions, and Declarations on Matters of Faith and Morals.* 43rd ed. San Francisco: Ignatius.

Derrida, J. (1997) *Of Grammatology.* Baltimore: Johns Hopkins University Press.

Duby, S. J. (2016) *Divine Simplicity.* London: Bloomsbury.

Efird, D., and Worsley, D. (2017) "What an Apophaticist Can Know: Divine Ineffability and the Beatific Vision," *Philosophy and Theology*, 29(2), pp. 205–217.

Eshleman, A. (2005) "Can an Atheist Believe in God?," *Religious Studies*, 41, pp. 195–214.

Evans, C. S. (2010) *Natural Signs and Knowledge of God: A New Look at Theistic Arguments.* Oxford: Oxford University Press.

Evans, C. S. (2013) *God and Moral Obligation.* Oxford: Oxford University Press.

Hauerwas, S. (2001) *With the Grain of the Universe: The Church's Witness and Natural Theology.* Grand Rapids, MI: Brazos.

Hick, J. (2000) "Ineffability," *Religious Studies*, 36(1), p. 35.

Horan, D. (2014) *Postmodernity and Univocity: A Critical Account of Radical Orthodoxy and John Duns Scotus.* Minneapolis, MN: Fortress Press.

Hume, D. (1998) *Dialogues Concerning Natural Religion.* New York: Hackett.

Hunsinger, G. (1993) "Truth as Self-Involving: Barth and Lindbeck on the Cognitive and Performative Aspects of Truth in Theological Discourse," *Journal of American Academy of Religion*, 61(1), pp. 41–56.

Hütter, R. (2011) "Attending to the Wisdom of God – from Effect to Cause, from Creation to God: A "Relecture" of the Analogy of Being according to

Thomas Aquinas," in White, T. J. (ed.) *The Analogy of Being: Invention of the Antichrist or Wisdom of God?* Grand Rapids, MI: Eerdmans, pp. 209–245.

Jacobs, J. (2015) "The Ineffable, Inconceivable, and Incomprehensible God: Fundamentality and Apophatic Theology," in Kvanvig, J. L. (ed.) *Oxford Studies in Philosophy of Religion Volume 6.* Oxford: Oxford University Press, pp. 158–176.

Johnson, K. (2010) *Karl Barth and Analogia Entis.* London: T & T Clark.

Kaufman, G. (1981) *The Theological Imagination: Constructing the Concept of God.* Philadelphia, PA: Westminster John Knox Press.

Keller, L. J. (2018) "Divine Ineffability and Franciscan Knowledge," *Res Philosophica*, 95(3), pp. 347–370.

Kimel, A. F. (ed.) (2001) *This Is My Name Forever: The Trinity & Gender Language for God.* New Haven, CT: IVP Academic.

Knepper, T. D. (2009) "Three Misuses of Pseudo-Dionysius for Comparative Theology," *Religious Studies*, 45(2), pp. 205–221.

Knepper, T. D. (2012) "Ineffability Now and Then: The Legacy of Neoplatonic Ineffability in Twentieth-Century Philosophy of Religion," *Quaestiones Disputatae*, 2, pp. 263–276.

Knepper, T. D. (2014) *Negating Negation. Against the Apophatic Abandonment of the Dionysian Corpus.* Eugene, OR: Cascade.

Kripke, S. (1972) "Naming and Necessity," in Davidson, D., and Harman, G. (eds.) *Semantics of Natural Language.* Dordrecht: Reidel, pp. 253–355. doi:10.1111/j.1468-0149.1981.tb02709.x.

Kügler, P. (2005) "The Meaning of Mystical 'Darkness,'" *Religious Studies*, 41, pp. 95–105.

Lebens, R. R. (2014) "Why So Negative about Negative Theology? The Search for a Plantinga-proof Apophaticism," *International Journal of Philosophy of Religion*, 76, pp. 259–275.

Legare, C., and Visala, A. (2011) "Between Religion and Science: Integrating Psychological and Philosophical Accounts of Explanatory Coexistence," *Human Development*, 54(3), pp. 169–184.

Lewin, D., Podmore, S. D., and Williams, D. (eds.) (2017) *Mystical Theology and Continental Philosophy: Interchange in the Wake of God.* London: Routledge.

Lindbeck, G. A. (2004) "George Lindbeck Replies to Avery Cardinal Dulles," *First Things* (January): 13–15.

Lindbeck, G. A. (2007) *The Nature of Doctrine: Religion and Theology in a Postliberal Age.* 25th anniversary edition. Louisville, KY: Westminster John Knox Press.

Lipton, P. (2007) "Science and Religion: The Immersion Solution," in Moore, A., and Scott, M. (eds.) *Realism and Religion: Philosophical and Theological Perspectives*. Aldershot: Ashgate.

Long, D. S. (2009) *Speaking of God: Theology, Language and Truth*. Grand Rapids, MI: Eerdmans.

Long, D. S. (2014) *Saving Karl Barth: Hans Urs von Balthasar's Preoccupation*. Minneapolis, MN: Fortress Press.

Long, S. A. (2011) *Analogia entis: On the Analogy of Being, Metaphysics, and the Act of Faith*. Notre Dame, IN: University of Notre Dame Press.

Luther, M. (2016) *The Bondage of the Will, 1525: The Annotated Luther*. Minneapolis, MN: Fortress Press.

MacIntyre, A. (2005) *Edith Stein: A Philosophical Prologue*. London: Continuum.

Maimonides, M. (1963) *Guide for the Perplexed. Transl. by Shlomo Pines*. Chicago: University of Chicago Press.

McCall, T. (2015) *Invitation to Christian Analytic Theology*. Downers Grove, IL: IVP.

McClendon, J. V., and Smith, J. M. (1973) "Ian Ramsey's Model of Religious Language: A Qualified Appreciation," *Journal of the American Academy of Religion*, 41(3), pp. 413–424.

McFague, S. (2013) *Collected Readings*. Edited by D. B. Lott. Minneapolis, MN: Fortress Press.

McGrath, A. E. (2002) *A Scientific Theology 2: Reality*. Edinburgh: T&T Clark. Available at: http://helka.linneanet.fi/cgi-bin/Pwebrecon.cgi?BBID=1846563.

McGraw, C. (2008) "The Realism/Anti-Realism Debate in Religion," *Philosophy Compass*, 3, pp. 254–272.

Mill, H. S. (1998) *Three Essays on Religion*. Amherst, NY: Prometheus Books.

Moore, A. (2013) "Theological Critiques of Natural Theology," in Manning, R. R. (ed.) *The Oxford Handbook of Natural Theology*. Oxford: Oxford University Press, pp. 227–246.

Neuner, J. (ed.) (1982) *The Christian Faith in the Documents of the Catholic Church*. Bangalore: Theological Publications in India.

Ortlund, G. (2014) "Divine Simplicity in Historical Perspective: Resourcing a Contemporary Discussion," *International Journal of Systematic Theology*, 16(4), pp. 436–453.

Philipse, H. (2012) *God in the Age of Science?: A Critique of Religious Reason*. Oxford: Oxford University Press.

Phillips, D. Z. (1976) *Religion without Explanation*. Oxford: Blackwell.

Phillips, D. Z. (2002) "Propositions, Pictures and Practices," *Ars Disputandi*, 2(1), pp. 161–174.

Plantinga, A. (2000) *Warranted Christian Belief.* New York: Oxford University Press.

Plantinga, A. (2015) *Knowledge and Christian Faith.* Grand Rapids, MI: Eerdmans.

Poidevin, R. le (1996) *Arguing for Atheism.* London: Routledge.

Poidevin, R. le (2019) *Religious Fictionalism.* Cambridge: Cambridge University Press.

Pouivet, R. (2011) "Against Theological Fictionalism," *European Journal for Philosophy of Religion*, 3, pp. 427–437.

Przywara, E. (2014) *Analogia entis: Metaphysics: Original Structure and Universal Rhythm.* Grand Rapids, MI: Eerdmans.

Pseudo-Dionysius (1987) "The Mystical Theology," in *Complete Works.* New York: Paulist Press.

Ramsey, I. T. (1957) *Religious Language.* Norwich: SCM Press.

Rauser, R. D. (2009) *Theology in Search of Foundations.* Oxford: Oxford University Press.

Rea, M. C. (2009) "Introduction," in Crisp, O., and Rea, M. C. (eds.) *Analytic Theology.* Oxford: Oxford University Press.

Rea, M. C. (2013) "Gender as a Divine Attribute," *Religious Studies*, 52(1), pp. 1–17.

Ritchie, A. (2012) *From Morality to Metaphysics. The Theistic Implications of Our Ethical Commitments.* Oxford: Oxford University Press.

Ross, J. F. (1981) *Portraying Analogy.* Cambridge: Cambridge University Press.

Saarinen, R. (1994) *Weakness of the Will in Medieval Thought: From Augustine to Buridan.* Leiden: Brill.

Sauchelli, A. (2016) "The Will to Make-Believe: Religious Fictionalism, Religious Beliefs, and the Value of Art," *Philosophy and Phenomenological Research*, 96(3), pp. 620–635.

Schroeder, M. (2008) "What Is the Frege-Geach Problem?," *Philosophy Compass*, 3(4), pp. 703–720.

Scott, D. (2016) *The Love That Made Mother Teresa.* Bedford, NH: Sophia Institute Press.

Scott, M. (2013) *Religious Language.* London: Palgrave Macmillan.

Scott, M., and Citron, G. (2016) "What Is Apophaticism? Ways of Talking about an Ineffable God," *European Journal for Philosophy of Religion*, 8(4), pp. 23–49.

Scott, M., and Malcolm, F. (2018) "Religious Fictionalism," *Philosophy Compass*, 13, pp. 1–11.

Sells, M. A. (1994) *Mystical Languages of Unsaying.* Chicago: The University of Chicago Press.

Sheridan, M. (2015) *Language for God in Patristic Tradition*. Downers Grove, IL: IVP Academic.

Smith, J. K. A. (2005) *Jacques Derrida: Live Theory*. London: Continuum.

Sober, E. (2019) *The Design Argument*. Cambridge: Cambridge University Press.

Sonderegger, K. (2015) *Systematic Theology. Volume 1, The Doctrine of God*. Minneapolis, MN: Fortress Press.

Soskice, J. M. (1985) *Metaphor and Religious Language*. Oxford: Clarendon Press.

Soskice, J. M. (2008) *The Kindness of God: Metaphor, Gender, and Religious Language*. Oxford: Oxford University Press.

Spinoza, B. (2007) *Theological-Political Treatise*. Cambridge: Cambridge University Press.

Springs, J. A. (2010) *Towards a Generous Orthodoxy*. Oxford: Oxford University Press.

Stein, E. (2000a) *On the Problem of Empathy*. Washington, DC: ICS Publications.

Stein, E. (2000b) 'Ways to Know God', in *Edith Stein, Knowledge and Faith*. Translated by Walter Redmond. Washington, DC: ICS Publications, pp. 83–145.

Stein, E. (2002) *Finite and Eternal Being*. Translated by Kurt F. Reinhardt. Washington, DC: ICS Publications.

Stein, E. (2003) *Science of the Cross*. Washington, DC: ICS Publications.

Stein, E. (2010) *Aus dem Leben einer jüdischen Familie und weitere autobiographische Beiträge*. Freiburg im Bresgau: Herder.

Stiver, D. R. (1996) *Philosophy of Religious Language: Sign, Symbol and Story*. Oxford: Blackwell.

Swinburne, R. (2008) *Revelation: From Metaphor to Analogy*. 2nd edition. Oxford: Oxford University Press.

Swinburne, R. (2014) *The Existence of God*. Oxford: Clarendon Press.

Swinburne, R. (2016) *The Coherence of Theism*. Second Edition. Oxford: Oxford University Press.

Tanner, N. P. 1990. *Decrees of the Ecumenical Councils*. 2 vols. Washington, DC: Georgetown University Press.

Ticciati, S. (2013) *A New Apophaticism: Augustine and the Redemption of Signs*. Leiden: Brill.

Tillich, P. (1957) *Dynamics of Faith*. New York: Harper.

Torrance, J. B. (1997) *Worship, Community and the Triune God of Grace*. New Haven, CT: IVP Academic.

Volf, M. (ed.) (2017) *Do We Worship the Same God? Jews, Christians, and Muslims in Dialogue*. Grand Rapids, MI: Eerdmans.

Wahlberg, M. (2014) *Revelation as Testimony*. Grand Rapids, MI: Eerdmans.

Warner, M. (1989) *Philosophical Finesse. Studies in the Art of Rational Persuasion*. Oxford: Clarendon Press.

Weed, J. H. (2018) "Religious Language," *Internet Encyclopedia of Philosophy*.

Weintraub, R. (2003) "Verificationism Revisited," *Ratio*, 16, pp. 83–98.

Westphal, M. (2001) *Overcoming Ontotheology*. New York: Fordham University Press.

White, R. M. (2010) *Talking about God: The Concept of Analogy and the Problem of Religious Language*. Lanham: Ashgate.

White, T. J. (ed.) (2010) *The Analogy of Being: Invention of the Antichrist or Wisdom of God?* Grand Rapids, MI: Eerdmans.

Williams, T. (2005) "The Doctrine of Univocity Is True and Salutary," *Modern Theology*, 21, pp. 575–585.

Wolterstoff, N. (2009) "How Philosophical Theology Became Possible within the Analytic Tradition of Philosophy," in Crisp, O. D., and Rea, M. C. (eds.) *Analytic Theology*. Oxford: Oxford University Press, pp. 155–170.

Yadaav, S. (2016) "Mystical Experience and the Apophatic Attitude," *Journal of Analytic Theology*, 4, pp. 17–43.

Yandell, K. E. (2013) "Religious Language," in Taliaferro, C., Harrison, V. S., and Goetz, S. (eds.) *The Routledge Companion to Theism*. London: Routledge, pp. 355–368.

Acknowledgments

I have benefited greatly from discussions with Max Baker-Hytch, D. Stephen Long, Ryan Mullins, Antti Mustakallio, Ben Page, Aku Visala, and Chris Woznicki. Special thanks are due to Lluis Oviedo, who enabled me to write parts of this Element at the Pontifical University Antonianum, Rome. The anonymous referee offered advice, which helped me to improve the text a great deal. All remaining mistakes are, of course, my own.

In Section 2.3, I have used parts of my previous published article "Dark Light: Mystical Theology of St. Edith Stein" (*Journal of Analytic Theology* 2016: 4). Published with permission.

Cambridge Elements $^{\equiv}$

Philosophy of Religion

Yujin Nagasawa

University of Birmingham

Yujin Nagasawa is Professor of Philosophy and Co-Director of the John Hick Centre for Philosophy of Religion at the University of Birmingham. He is currently President of the British Society for the Philosophy of Religion. He is a member of the Editorial Board of *Religious Studies*, the *International Journal for Philosophy of Religion* and *Philosophy Compass*.

About the Series

This Cambridge Elements series provides concise and structured introductions to all the central topics in the philosophy of religion. It offers balanced, comprehensive coverage of multiple perspectives in the philosophy of religion. Contributors to the series are cutting-edge researchers who approach central issues in the philosophy of religion. Each provides a reliable resource for academic readers and develops new ideas and arguments from a unique viewpoint.

Cambridge Elements ☰

Philosophy of Religion

A full series listing is available at: www.cambridge.org/EPREL

Printed in the United States
By Bookmasters